Life with the Robins and Beyond

NEIL PALMER

Life with the Robins and Beyond

THE GEOFF MERRICK STORY

pitch

First published by Pitch Publishing, 2022

Pitch Publishing
A2 Yeoman Gate
Yeoman Way
Worthing
Sussex
BN13 3QZ
www.pitchpublishing.co.uk
info@pitchpublishing.co.uk

A CIP catalogue record is available for this book from the British Library.

ISBN 978 1 80150 062 3

Typesetting and origination by Pitch Publishing

Printed and bound in Great Britain by TJ Books Ltd.

Contents

This book is dedicated to my lovely wife Wendy, my beautiful children Charlie, Elliott and Luke, my brother Vernon, his wife Jill and their family, and of course my mum and dad, who were the most wonderful parents that a man could ever want.

Acknowledgements

MANY PEOPLE have been important to me in my life and career, and I expect they don't realise just how much they have done. I have mentioned many people in the book and I also wanted to thank others. They are, in no particular order, Neil Palmer, Alan Dicks, Dave Fear, Richard Scudamore, Andrew Urch and family, Rex Baker, Danny Baker, George Baker, Rich Dyer, Jeff Nash, Pat Fitzgerald, Ray Kenny, Joe Royle and the whole of the Bristol City promotion squad of 1975/76.

Foreword

IT REALLY is an honour to say a few words about my friend Geoff Merrick.

I arrived at Bristol City in 1977 and at the time the Robins were in the First Division and looking for a striker with a bit of experience. I joined from Manchester City and if I'm honest, at first I never really wanted to leave Maine Road but opportunities there were limited for me. Geoff was a fantastic guy who along with his family made myself and my family extremely welcome as our new adventure unfolded.

Things were a bit of a shock at first as the club did not have the greatest training facilities and they had only just installed a laundry room to get our kit washed, which was a far cry from Manchester City. I remember Geoff telling me, 'This is how it is, Joe, so I suggest you just get on with it,' which I certainly did, and looking back I suppose that was the charm of the place along with the incredible team spirit the lads had.

That spirit had a lot to do with Geoff, Gerry Gow, Gerry Sweeney, Tom Ritchie and of course Geoff's great pal Chris Garland, and I felt extremely privileged to be let in to this close-knit bunch of friends and be treated as one of their own.

They were a bunch of lads who played together and socialised together. I had had some great dressing rooms over my career, notably Everton and Manchester City, but the Bristol City one was certainly unique as all the lads were mates and this never changed when manager Alan Dicks brought in the likes of myself, Norman Hunter and Peter Cormack. We had all played for big clubs but we all bought into the way City did things.

I was aware of Geoff as a player before I signed and many people in the game thought he should be playing at a bigger club, which was meant with no disrespect to City but I know there was a lot of talk of clubs interested in him throughout his career. He was a great leader on and off the pitch, good in the air with an enormous leap, a great left foot and when it came to pace there were not many who could live with him. He was a natural centre-back.

You could see leading up to games, and also afterwards, how much the result and the club meant to him. Don't get me wrong, all the lads cared, but there was something within Geoff where you could see it meant everything to him. Maybe it was the fact that he was born a stone's throw from the ground and the people who went to the games were his people, and I think that is something that never left him.

It was testimony to his strength of character and love for the club that when he was moved to full-back on the arrival of

Norman Hunter – left-back wasn't his position – I know that he was far from happy but that never affected his relationship with Norman and it certainly never affected his loyalty to the club. Typical of Geoff, he just rolled his sleeves up and got on with things, very much putting the team first above his own feelings.

Off the field he has had some tough times that would have broken many people, but Geoff is a grafter and a solid guy who will always have my respect for the type of man he is and the type of family he and Wendy have created. We still keep in touch and I love coming down to Bristol for various functions that we have been invited to. I am really pleased that he has decided to write this book, as I know his story is certainly one that will cover all the emotions for the reader. As I said, it's an honour to be part of this wonderful man's story.

Joe Royle

Introduction

TO MANY people, Geoff Merrick will always be Mr Bristol City. From a fan's point of view he lived the dream: born within a stone's throw of Ashton Gate, he captained his country as a schoolboy and captained his beloved Robins through some of the club's greatest moments. Whether it was promotion to the First Division in 1975/76 or leading his team out at Highbury for their first game in football's top tier, Geoff carried every supporter with him as they knew he was one of their own.

He wasn't the star of that legendary promotion-winning side, I can vouch for the fact that kids in the school playgrounds at that time wanted to be the tough-tackling Gerry Gow or score the goals like Paul Cheesley or Tom Ritchie, but Geoff was in the engine room of that glorious team alongside the likes of Dave Rodgers, Brian Drysdale or Gerry Sweeney. They won the ball and stopped others playing and made the team tick, and at the very heart was Geoff.

On the pitch he leapt with springs in his feet; there were not many opponents who could beat him in the air. His left foot would unlock a pass with ultimate ease and his reading of the game would take out any striker regardless of reputations.

Let's also not forget that in a world where every team had their own hatchet men lurking in the back four or in midfield, Geoff could mix it with the best of them when necessary but everybody knew that wasn't his game. His reputation for a cool head and a measured tackle earned him the tag of the Second Division's Bobby Moore and it was something that fitted him perfectly.

Throughout his Bristol City career, his loyalty to the club remained strong as Arsenal and Wolverhampton Wanderers, to name but two, came calling for his signature. There was no interest from the man from Bedminster, citing on many occasions, 'Why would I leave Bristol City?' It was a loyalty that would cost him dearly in the end as the club unravelled through mis-management.

With the 1980s on the horizon, Geoff and seven other players tore up their contracts to save the club from going out of existence. What followed was a football mercenary existence as he played in Hong Kong and South Africa to keep a roof over his family's head, realising that he would never go back to playing in the Football League again. A successful building company followed but it was then ravaged by recession and to top it all, a health scare a few years ago proved that life has thrown many things at Geoff and his family and they have coped with all of them admirably.

My first meeting with this legend of Bristol City was on 11 November 1972. I was ten years old and walking outside the Williams Stand at Ashton Gate with my dad before the Robins played Queens Park Rangers in the Second Division. Walking towards me that day was Geoff Merrick in his legendary sheepskin coat on his way to the players' entrance. I instinctively stood in his way and from my parka coat I pulled out a biro and the match programme, which had a drawing of him on the front cover that season. 'Excuse me Mr Merrick, could you sign this for me?' I asked. 'Of course, son,' he replied, ruffling my hair as he finished the autograph for me. A small crowd gathered, eager to get his attention; as he moved on everyone shouted, 'Good luck Geoff,' and then he was gone. I was thrilled and I still have the programme to this day.

Fast-forward 35 years and that ten-year-old schoolboy is stood outside Geoff's Nailsea Farm house waiting for him to answer the door so I can interview him for my first book, *Bristol Derby Days*. My stomach was in knots as I so wanted to make a good impression on him.

Geoff opened the door and welcomed me in. I remember looking at him and thinking that he looked exactly the same as when he played for the club, except of course for the obligatory 1970s moustache which had long gone. I recalled the autograph story and typical of Geoff, he remarked how he hoped his signature did not spoil a perfectly good programme. From that day in 2007 I have interviewed Geoff and spent time in his company for various projects and seen at close hand how he has dealt with many of the hurdles he has had to face regarding his life. As I wrote in 2009, I have always felt it was wrong that he was remembered as somebody who was caught up in the mis-management of a football club rather than celebrating his career. He told me at the time that he gets criticised for mentioning the 'Ashton Gate Eight' affair, but that's all reporters or the media ask him about so he can't win.

Whenever I have interviewed him our talks have gone on beyond the initial discussion and we have spoken about all sorts of aspects of modern-day football and of course his life in general. I have always thought he should write a book but knowing Geoff as I do, he is the sort of man who is very low key, like his dad was. He is someone who never pushes himself forward as he would say to me, 'I can't write a book, Neil, nobody would be interested in me,' which I always found baffling considering the wave of affection for him from supporters of both Bristol clubs.

We spoke at length regarding the Gerry Gow biography that I was working on and I mentioned how sad it was that somebody was not able to sit down with Gerry before he passed away and get his thoughts down on paper. I'm not sure whether it struck a chord with Geoff but I soon heard from his son Luke, who told me that his dad thought the time was right for the book to happen.

We met to discuss it and he told me that he would do a book and put every part of his life in. Regarding the Ashton Gate Eight affair, he told me that he would give fans the truth and leave it up to them to have their own opinions as to the rights and wrongs of the situation. He was adamant that once he poured it all out he was putting the whole situation to bed in terms of talking about it. We agreed and away we went, meeting every Wednesdays admittedly by phone for the majority of the book due to lockdown restrictions.

During the course of the writing process Geoff has been honest and at times there have been laughs and tears which I hope are reflected in the pages of this book. I have been overwhelmed by his honesty. He has opened up about various things in his life that even he has admitted he just pushed to the back of his mind for years and never dealt with. He has talked about depression and anxiety and I'm reminded of the ancient Chinese philosopher Lao Tzu, who said, 'Leadership is the ability to hide your panic from others.' At times during his career this sums Geoff up to a tee.

I also cannot thank Geoff and his wonderful family of Wendy, Charlie, Luke and Elliott enough for letting me into their tight-knit group. Again, their honesty and openness to tell Geoff's story was remarkable and I thank them from the bottom of my heart.

As for Geoff, well I have been in the company of many footballers over the years, some of whom are keen to tell you their achievements and sometimes the fame they once enjoyed has led to an arrogance about them, but not this Bedminster boy. He has a calmness about him and a dignity that many people can learn from. He is still that lad from Garnett Street and he never lost that ability to connect with all sorts of people in any walk of life.

I'm eternally grateful that he asked this one-time ten-year-old autograph-hunter to have the responsibility of telling his story. It's a responsibility that I take on with immense pride and with a certain amount of trepidation; after all, Geoff Merrick is a very special man who will be etched into the very fabric of Bristol City Football Club forever.

Neil Palmer

1
Bedminster Boy

OVER THE years, I have been asked many times to write a book. The requests have come from fans, journalists I have met during my career and even family members. I always said no, mainly because I was not sure that anybody would be interested in my story. It is a trait in my nature that I probably inherited from my dad. I suppose I am just not very big in putting myself forward and being in the limelight; strange for a footballer, I know, and especially a captain, but that's just the way I am.

As a kid I was really shy and the area I grew up in and the people I lived among were not the type to bare their soul and show off as it were, mainly due to the fact that we didn't have anything to show off about, but it also kept you grounded and taught you not to get too big for your boots and I think I carried that around with me through adult life. So, as I have now said yes to the book, I hope you will get to know and understand a little bit more about Geoff Merrick the footballer and the man.

Looking back at my career and my life I can see that there is a tale to tell. I was a local lad who captained his hometown club to football's top flight. The way it all ended for me is a book all on its own but painful though it was, I came through it with the love and support of my family and some dear friends.

So why did I say yes? I have known writer Neil Palmer for around 15 years. We first met when he interviewed me for one of his books and we just seemed to get on. Neil always asked me about a book, particularly as we have kept in touch since that first meeting, and it was when he interviewed me for his biography on my old team-mate and friend Gerry Gow that I started to think about it. Neil said that he was saddened that he couldn't sit down with Gerry and talk about his life and career due to his passing. He made it clear that, heaven forbid anything happened to me, then somebody somewhere would write about my career and life so maybe it would be best to at least do a book, to put a few records straight in terms of my career but more importantly for my family, especially my grandchildren – Harvey, Brooke, Lewis, Ethan, Daniel, Emilia, Mia and Olivia – so they could see that grandad did once play football and also they can find out a bit more about the life I have lived.

I have enjoyed the experience of going over my life and remembering some people who were close to my heart and certain events that meant so much to me. In truth, I have found it very cathartic as I grow older. I have also been able to find loads of things relating to my career that I thought I had lost over the years due to my rummaging about in the loft at home. So I said yes to Neil and here it is, a story of a lad from Bedminster whose dream came true.

I was told by my mother that I came into this world during a snowstorm. I always told her that in my life it has been snowing ever since. She gave birth to me in a bedroom at 89 Garnett Street, Bedminster, Bristol, on 29 April 1951. I'm not sure who else was there but my dad and elder brother Vernon were keeping out of the way while Geoffrey Merrick was arriving into the world.

My parents were the most wonderful people and as they say in Bedminster they were 'proper'. Dad was Herbert Edgar; the best dad anyone could ask for, he was an unassuming man who never pushed himself to the front of things. He was always in the background with his fag in the corner of his mouth and that suited him. Dad was a carpenter by trade and he initially worked all over the country making and erecting greenhouses. Being the family man he was he soon got tired of going here, there and everywhere and missing his family, so he got a job with the Ministry of Defence based at Whitening Yard, about 15 minutes' walk from our house. He was still doing carpentry and told me once that he made some toilet cubicles on a site that the Queen was visiting. He was very honoured to have been asked to do it but apparently the Queen never used the loo and he had to dismantle them, making sure that the loo seat was destroyed in case somebody stole it and sold it.

Mum again was the most wonderful mother you could have asked for. Her name was Iris Florence, although Dad called her Flo. She kept house and it was spotless; occasionally she would earn a few quid cleaning at the John Collier clothing store on East Street in Bedminster.

Making up the Merrick family household was my brother Vernon, who is ten years older than me. Although there was a significant age gap, Vernon and myself were really close. He went to Bristol Grammar School and did well at rugby and cricket. He joined the army and worked in the intelligence corps, becoming fluent in Russian. He really was a James Bond character, being lowered from helicopters on to submarines during his service. Today he lives in Leicester and we talk on the phone frequently. As a brother I couldn't have asked for better.

Home for the Merricks was Garnett Street. It was a terraced house with three bedrooms, a kitchen and front room. Our home was situated on top of a hill, which was brilliant fun for a youngster on a bike like me coming down, but I moaned every time I rode up it, wishing and muttering under my breath that we lived on a flat road.

The streets were where me and my mates played. We were out there from dawn until dusk playing football, riding our bikes or playing a game called 'Kicked In', which meant leaving a ball or a tin in the middle of the road, a lad would be 'it' and you and your friends would all hide and he would have to come and look for you. While he was searching, if you got the chance you would run out of your hiding place and kick the ball before he got there. We loved it, as did the local glazing firm which was kept busy replacing the odd pane of glass across Bedminster.

We would also play football on a bit of land called the Marsh. I used to drive my mum crazy as I would come home from a game of football covered in mud from head to toe. Mum used to say, 'Where have you been? Look at the state of your clothes.' You have to bear in mind that I didn't have that many clothes as we were poor like a lot of families around the area, but the one thing my clothes were when I wore them was clean and tidy.

Mum would say, 'Why can't you be more like Geoffrey Fleming?' Geoffrey was my best friend and we did loads together. His mum and dad had a bit more money than mine and they lived in a big house. I always remember he had a fantastic toboggan that his dad made him and we would go hurtling down Garnett Street at about 50 miles an hour in the snow. The thing with Geoffrey, which so impressed my mum, was that despite us playing football or doing all sorts he always came back immaculately dressed without a speck of mud on him whereas I was covered from head to toe.

I loved those days and I have always loved Bedminster as an area. It was a real community where everybody seemed to know each other and everybody seemed to look after each other. It was home to WH Wills, makers of tobacco which they exported all over the world, and they were also the main employers in south Bristol. Their huge red-brick buildings dominated the skyline along with Ashton Gate, the home of Bristol City Football Club. From nearly every view in Bedminster you could see the ground, and for us youngsters it was a magical place. Everybody supported the team; my mum and dad were ardent fans as well as all our neighbours, and you just couldn't support anybody else.

Us youngsters used to go to watch the Robins every other Saturday, but we made sure we got there at half-time as then the men on the turnstiles would let you in free to watch the second half. Me and my friends loved it watching these superstars playing in the red shirts of City: men like John Atyeo, Mike Threasher and Gordon Parr, although the list is endless, and we would also be amazed when we saw them around the area. They were like gods to us all. You're so impressionable when you're young and if these men waved or said hello, which they often did, you would remember it for your whole life. I certainly have done.

Bristol City were languishing in the Second Division and managed by Pat Beasley, but to be honest we didn't care who was in charge or where in the league they were – to us they were the greatest team in the world. I always loved football and my dad, who was a good local player by all accounts who turned out for South Bristol Central, always encouraged me to play but if I'm honest I never had any real aspirations as I never thought somebody like me could become a player. I also thought that I wasn't really any better than any of my mates.

My first real inroads to football came at Luckwell Infant School, which was about a five-minute walk from our house. It was an old Victorian building which at the time I thought was huge but looking at it now, it's plainly not the big place I thought it was. There I came under the watchful eye of two teachers I have never forgotten, Mrs Gibbs and Mr Prewitt. They both encouraged me and also taught me about the game and what was expected of you in terms of fair play and sportsmanship. Both were strict and tough but they had something about them that just made you want to learn from them.

Mrs Gibbs took us for exercise and she was the one who taught me how to play football properly, taking time with me and my mates on explaining how to strike a ball correctly. Mr Prewitt also took PE and he along with Mrs Gibbs encouraged the young Geoff Merrick to play for the school football team. Back then the schools league was a really well organised affair with league tables printed in the local paper and a list of fixtures, which considering I would have been about seven years old was an amazing amount of detail for school football. Our games were on a Saturday morning so me and my school-mates, the ones who lived nearby, all met up at the Luckwell Hotel round the corner from the school and got the 22 bus across the city to our fixture. We always got the 22 as it nearly always took us to where we wanted to go in Bristol, and if it fell short we just walked the rest of the way.

I loved playing outfield although at one time I really fancied myself as a goalkeeper, and on a few occasions I played in goal for the school. My favourite player was Tony Macedo, who was Fulham's goalkeeper. I thought he was brilliant and decided that goalkeeper was the position for me until Mr Prewitt and my dad had a gentle word in my ear about how the team needed me outfield. I wished I had gone against their advice in a local derby against South Street School, who were just up the road from us. Mr Prewitt gave us a little team talk and warned me of their star player, a blond lad called Chris Garland. Mr Prewitt told me to watch Chris as he was an exceptionally good player. Chris was two years older than me and he lived in Ashton, which was right next to Bedminster, and although I cannot remember the result I do remember he ran rings round me that day and when we tussled for the ball, he punched me in the eye. Chris would become one of my great friends on and off the pitch; we shared some great times and some not-so-great times together at Bristol City and he will always be special to me.

I did well with Luckwell but as I said I never really had any thoughts of being a professional player. Mr Prewitt, however, believed in me and put me forward for the Bristol Boys trial at Bower Ashton, which was just up the road. The Bristol Boys had various age groups and they would play against other teams from different towns and cities. It was really prestigious to be selected as many lads who were picked through the years became professional players. I was about 11 and did well enough to get in the team.

Running alongside the football was another love of mine, which for a lad in the middle of Bristol seemed strange – farming. I remember me and my mate Bob Locke walked to Lower Ashton, which was a few miles away, where there was a piece of land called Parsonage Farm, owned by the Withes family. We knocked on the door and asked if we could do some work on the farm and the owner Les said, 'Yes, of course.' He said he would pay us five shillings a day so we were well chuffed. We loved it and at 12 I was driving tractors around. When Les wanted me to drive the tractor he would put one of his old coats on me along with his flat cap, so if anyone saw me they thought there was a thin old man driving the tractor. I don't think Health & Safety was invented then, not that we would have paid much attention to it.

This was a love that stayed with me all my life. I worked at Parsonage until I was 21 and then worked for another lovely guy called Joe Baker at his farm. I did all this alongside my football career and loved it. Pre-season and through the summer was hard work but I felt all the better for it. I have always been happier outdoors and it's a side of my life not many people know about.

Football was kicking in for me but something was looming on the horizon that could have easily scuppered my future career – the 11-plus exam. This was introduced in 1944 by the government as a selective process designed to direct pupils to grammar school or secondary school. You had one attempt, and the exam consisted of Maths and English. My dilemma centred around the fact that grammar schools only played rugby whereas secondary schools played football. So my choices were to pass the exam and go to Ashton Park School to play rugby or fail and go to Southville School and play football.

I was quite honest about what I wanted to do, and that was to fail the exam, leaving me to play the game I loved. It shows the love my parents had for me as they knew and told me to do what made me happy. I really don't think there were many kids at that time whose parents would have been happy with their son failing but it shows how special they were. My head teacher, Miss Withers, was so against me failing that she tried to get me to go to Horticultural College but it would have been residential so that was never going to happen.

I took the exam and I remember when the results came through, me and Mum gripped the envelope and gingerly opened it. I was so nervous I couldn't focus, and then Mum took the paper, looked at it, and said, 'You have failed.' With that we jumped around the room. Looking back, it was a bizarre situation to have been told that I had failed and for those words to bring on such joy in the Merrick household.

I arrived at Southville School happy that my football would continue. The school was only a couple of minutes' walk from our house so again it was perfect for me. At Southville, I again came under the influence of some great teachers who made a real mark on my life, such as Vernon Templar and Dick Williamson. Mr Williamson was also a Bristol Boys selector and both men had a massive influence on my life. I was still playing for Bristol Boys and I remember Bristol City having 'open' games at Ashton Gate where kids could turn up and see if they could get a few minutes in the trial. I went along with my friends, mainly so we could have a game on a proper pitch, and I must have impressed with my few minutes as they asked me to sign a schoolboy form.

The form never really registered with me. I was happy playing with my mates and of course I was thrilled that City were interested, as were my parents, but I had the philosophy that people like me don't become footballers. It's interesting looking back now but although I was a Bristol City schoolboy I never attended the ground for any coaching. In fact they didn't have an awful lot to do with me, and how it went couldn't be any further from today's football when lads join academies for intense coaching at around nine years of age or younger.

I continued to progress with Southville and our team made it to the final of the Woodcock Shield, a knockout tournament for school teams across Bristol and very prestigious to win. It was introduced in 1907 by Herbert Woodcock who was alderman to the council in Bristol. He believed in sport for young people and thought a competitive football tournament would be good for the schools. Our final was played at Ashton Gate and we were thrilled to be on the same pitch as the one our heroes used. We played Hartcliffe School and drew 2-2, with our two goals coming from a lad who joined from South Street by the name of Chris Garland. I was just glad to have Chris on my team rather than against us. Even at an early age you could see he was a real talent and for us he was somebody we all looked up to.

The two schools shared the shield for six months each and it was a brilliant feeling to be lifting a trophy at the home of my beloved Bristol City. So, there I was lifting a trophy at Ashton Gate and a Bristol City schoolboy, so surely things could not get any better? If only I knew what was round the corner.

2
Feet on the Ground

YOU HAVE noticed that I don't really talk about any academic subjects that I enjoyed during my time at school. That's mainly due to the fact that I didn't really enjoy any. I have told you I failed my 11-plus and I am not sure whether I failed it deliberately or I wasn't bright enough to pass it in the first place, so perhaps we will never know?

After Southville School's performance in the Woodcock Shield we became the centre of attention locally and there were various write-ups in the local paper regarding us all, which was great, but we all had people around us who would keep our feet on the ground and tell us about the importance of school work. Remember, I was also still working when I could at the local farm and that was bloody hard graft for a 14-year-old so it concentrated your mind. I can't stress the importance of having good people around. My mum and dad encouraged me in everything I wanted to do, and as I mentioned, at school and through my football I had people like Vernon Templar and Dick Williamson and others who you will read about in this book who taught me so much.

Dick, for example, built me up and taught me how to be a man and give respect, and he gave me an insight into life. He didn't really coach me, he encouraged me, and it's a wonderful thing to know that people believe in what you are doing, especially for a young and impressionable 14-year-old. Dick would say, 'When you play, roll up your sleeves. It will make you stand out no matter what the weather. It makes you look ready and opponents and anyone watching will notice you.' He also instilled discipline on the field and how the referee's word is final, even if you don't agree with it. You should always show respect to his position and it was something I never forgot and used throughout my career.

Vernon was the same. I listened intently when he gave advice and encouragement. Watching today's football, a lot of players need a Dick Williamson or Vernon Templar in their early life, particularly when looking at their antics with referees. Both men pushed me towards having a trial for England Schoolboys and the main man there was Ted King, who was based in Bristol and was a selector. Ted was also in charge of Bristol Boys and under his stewardship we had a great run in the English Schools Trophy. I was captain of the side and I remember we beat Bournemouth at Eastville, Bristol Rovers' ground, then we met Liverpool in the quarter-finals and beat them 1-0 after a couple of draws. This set up a two-legged semi-final against East London Boys. We beat them 1-0 in the first leg at Millwall's Den then unfortunately lost the return 3-0 at Eastville, where a lad called Tony Carr really did put us to the sword. Tony went on to play for West Ham

United and ended up as the director of youth development at the club, bringing through the likes of Frank Lampard, Joe Cole and Rio Ferdinand. We were all bitterly disappointed to have lost but getting so far in the competition really made us all hungry for more success.

One of the lads in that Bristol Boys team was Ian Broomfield. Ian was a great lad and a very talented player; he and I were invited to Bisham Abbey in High Wycombe, which was a large stately home with fantastic football pitches and facilities. It was the England football team's base and we were chosen among other lads for the selectors to look at with a view to getting into the England Schoolboys team. Our time was taken up with games and really good coaching. It was residential, so Ian and I went for two weeks in the summer and we loved every minute of it. After the initial two weeks I was chosen for a trial game, South-West v South-East, so I went with Ted to Cricklefield Athletic Ground in Redbridge. I wasn't particularly nervous and that had a lot to do with Ted, who by his very nature was relaxed. I had a good game and I know this sounds crazy but I just thought of it as another match.

After that game there was a fixture between South and North teams at Vicarage Road, Watford's ground. What is amazing looking back at the programmes and articles I have at home, which I dug out for this book, is the list of players who were at Bisham Abbey with me but never got picked for the England games that year. Players of the calibre of Peter Shilton, Charlie

George, Tony Currie, Phil Neal, Peter Spiring and Tony Carr were all great footballers and some of them went to the very top of the game, but I'm sure at the end of the trial they were broken-hearted and probably told by parents or coaches to never stop trying. It just shows you must never give up on your dreams, as football is all about opinions at the time.

On the way home, Ted said, 'By the way, they picked you.' I didn't really react and I didn't really believe it, so we just carried on driving and Ted said no more about it. When I got home, my parents asked how it went and I just said I played well and that was that but all the time I kept thinking, 'He did say they picked you,' but I was probably too afraid to say anything to my parents and my mates in case I had got it wrong. I know some kids would have come bursting through the door shouting 'I have been picked' but as I have said before, that really wasn't my way.

I didn't have to wait long as a few days later I was doing my paper round for Percy Padgett, who had a newsagents. I was on East Street in Bedminster with my bike leant up against the NatWest Bank when I picked up a copy of the *Western Daily Press*, which was one of the local papers. I always read the sport on the back page of the paper while on the round. I looked at this headline towards the corner of the page and it said 'MERRICK PICKED FOR ENGLAND'. I looked at it again and sure enough, that's what it said. I read a bit more and it stated that local lad Geoff Merrick had been chosen for the forthcoming schoolboy internationals starting with the England v Ireland game at St Andrew's, Birmingham City's ground. I rolled the paper up, finished the round which thankfully was nearly over, and raced back to the shop. I burst in as the bell on the door nearly came off its bracket and clutching the paper I said to Percy, 'I can't believe it, I have been picked for England, look it's in the paper.' He grabbed me and gave me a hug and we both, along with a few other customers, read the piece again with everyone telling me well done.

I then took the paper, got on my bike and raced home, flying up that bloody Garnett Street hill. When I got inside and told my mum and dad they were bursting with pride. Looking back, it's a great memory to have of seeing both your parents so happy and proud over something you have done. It really will stay with me forever.

When everything died down, I was contacted through the post with news that I would be selected for England at under-16 level. Ted King then came to see me and told me that I was going to be captain for the series of games, which I couldn't believe. Everyone around the area was talking about it and wishing me well; my mates were really pleased for me as was the school. I appeared again in the local paper where they pointed out the last England schoolboy from Bristol was the brilliant winger Jantzen Derrick, who was playing at Bristol City and who I loved to watch. Jantzen had been the star of England Schoolboys some seven or eight years earlier and the papers loved to run the story of the two of us. I also found myself having a photo taken with Bristol City legend John Atyeo, himself a full England international in the 1950s. John was brilliant with me and he said some wonderful things in the newspapers about the big future I had in the game.

England Schoolboys were about to embark on a series of five games over the months of April and May, and had picked a collection of lads who would, with a few tweaks allowing for injury, be the team for all of the internationals. My debut was on 2 April 1966 at St Andrew's against Ireland. I went up the day before along with Ted King and the team stayed at a hotel, which was certainly something I had never done before. Ted gave my family the heads up and my mum explained to me beforehand that at dinner I should start with the cutlery from the outside and work in. From the FA, I was given trousers, a shirt, tie and a blazer with the three lions on. It really was a far cry from helping out with the cows on the farm, walking around the hotel dressed as a proper footballer.

The game went well and although as a team we had only just met, we played really well and clicked in a 1-0 win. I took it all in my stride and on the evening we had a large dinner with a few speeches and of course the handing out of the England Schoolboys caps. Back then, if you played for England you got a cap and even though there was a possibility I could be making more appearances throughout this run I would only get the one cap, which was policy at the time. After dinner they called out my name and up I went to receive my cap. I was so proud to get it and if you come to my house it's the only bit of memorabilia about my career that I have on display, along with my England shirt. It's really special to me. I arrived home and my parents and the neighbours couldn't wait to see me with the cap, all dressed up with my England blazer on.

No disrespect to any of the other countries involved or different venues but the jewel in the crown of the fixtures was England v West Germany at Wembley, which just happened to be the next game for us, and it was also the day before my 15th birthday. The year was 1966 and the World Cup would be starting in a few months at that very stadium. I have to say the hype certainly wasn't around like it is today for World Cups or any international tournament. Yes, there were posters around and the odd bit of merchandise such as the mascot World Cup Willie along with flags and rosettes, but it was still very low key.

The schoolboy team stayed in the Star and Garter Hotel in Richmond, which was situated on the River Thames and a short drive from the stadium. We loved it as we were treated like top-class footballers; they even sorted out a birthday cake for me which was brilliant. We travelled to Wembley on the coach and there were fans everywhere. When we arrived and got off the coach dressed in our England attire, there was a real buzz about us as we went into the dressing rooms. While we looked for our seats I had a couple of messages and telegrams. Among them were two from Dick Williamson and Vernon Templar wishing me well, and of course mum and dad.

Ted King and some of the selectors told us the side, which would be the same against Ireland: Stephen Bowtell, Alan Mitchell, David McLelland, Stephen Sargent, Paul Clarke, Geoffrey Merrick, Patrick Lowery, Lyndon Hughes, Stephen Wilkinson, Robert Allen and David Thomas, with Malcolm Webster, Robert Bell, Alan Moody, David Dangerfield and Anthony Hallan as the reserves. I remember them all with such affection. We all picked up a programme on our way out to walk the pitch with about an hour to go. In its pages it said of me that I was an 'excellent worker' and a 'first-class example to his team'. The programme also said that my heading and tackling were 'outstanding', which boosted my confidence no end.

It was during the walk around that the nerves really began to kick in. Even with an hour to go the place was almost full and I remember it being a boiling hot day, so I was sweating something terrible. The noise of the crowd was deafening and I scanned the terraces to see if I could see any family and friends, but it was just a block of colour and a wall of sound coming back at me. As 3pm approached I led the England team up the tunnel and suddenly we came into the warm sunshine and there was an unforgettable roar from the crowd. I felt my legs go a bit but I managed to compose myself. There was a crowd of 82,000 in the ground, an incredible attendance for a schoolboy international anyway, but back then the Wembley fixture was always the big one.

We lined up and were introduced to various dignitaries including Horace King, who was the speaker at the House of

Commons. I couldn't wait to get going and when we kicked off the lads played magnificently in the hot sunshine. We played like we had known each other for years and we went on to win 2-1. At the end of the game I had the honour of leading the team up the famous Wembley steps to collect our trophies. It was the most magical moment of my young life. Was it a premonition? Who knows; a blond defender with number six on his back leading an England team up the Wembley steps to receive a trophy after beating West Germany, surely that couldn't happen again, could it?

After the game the local press went to town regarding the young England captain, hyping me up no end. I was especially pleased to see a piece in the paper from ex-Bristol City and England forward John Atyeo who said that I 'had a wonderful game and could be the next Danny Blanchflower'. It was high praise indeed from a footballer I had always admired for the way he conducted himself on and off the field.

I took all of this in my stride and after the wonderful occasion of Wembley the team stayed together and travelled up to York City's ground some two days later to play the West Germans again. No disrespect to York or their Bootham Crescent stadium, but it was a far cry from Wembley with just a few thousand fans dotted around. But again we were on the winning team, beating the Germans 1-0.

After the games I had to go to school and all of Southville were immensely proud of my achievement, although there was no real word from Bristol City regarding my England appearances.

As Southville were so proud they asked me to come in with my England blazer and tie and appear at assembly. If I'm honest, it wasn't really my thing as when you're 15 all you want to do is blend in with your mates. That said, I knew how good everyone at Southville had been to me and I make no apologies to say I was really proud to captain England so I said yes to their request. I was called up at assembly and in general everybody was pleased for me, apart from one lad who took exception to the attention I was getting and he decided to start a fight with me in the playground. It was also unfortunate for me that he was twice my size and his blows rained down on me with all the kids watching. Before I ended up in hospital, Dick Williamson jumped in between us and pulled us apart. Dick then put me in his Morris Oxford car and promptly drove me home, making sure he had straightened my tie and brushed all the dirt off my England blazer and trousers and given me a tissue for my cut lip.

Dick knocked on the door and Mum opened it. She could see I was in a right state and asked us both what had happened. Before I said a word, Dick said, 'Sorry Mrs Merrick, your son has just duffed up the biggest kid in the school. He truly is amazing. I had to bring him home before he duffed up the kid's bigger brother.' That was Dick – he didn't want my mum to be upset regarding me being picked on and he wanted to build my confidence as well. There was no more fighting after that and I presume Dick went and had a word with the lad in question. It's funny but my attacker and I became good friends after that.

My next game for England was Wales at home and I could not have been any more thrilled to find out it was going to be at Ashton Gate. It was incredible to be using the very benches, bath and hooks that the Bristol City players used. All my family and friends came and the place made a hell of a noise as we won 3-1.

My final appearance in the three lions shirt was away to Scotland at Glasgow Rangers' Ibrox Stadium. I was with the team but my family, along with my new girlfriend Jenny who I'd met at Southville, drove up to the game in my dad's Ford Anglia. It just showed the level of support from them. The game was really tough and the Scots had a great lad up front who really gave me the run-around all afternoon. It ended 1-1 and I was pleased that the whole team had performed so well during the fixtures. At the dinner afterwards, I was sat next to the Scottish lad and asked him if he had a club sorted. He explained that he had quite a few offers but was happy to stay in Scotland. I asked his name and he said Kenneth Dalglish. Later in my career, Kenny gave me the run-around every time I played against him when we were pros, but he really was something that afternoon at Ibrox. His skill and touch were second to none.

And so my time as an England Schoolboys player came to an end. It's an incredible honour to be picked at international level as a schoolboy and, I would have been happy if my footballing journey had ended there. For many youngsters it is the peak of their career, and there have also been many future great players that never got to play at that level as youngsters. When I look at that team, eight of us, including me, went on to have footballing careers. The pick of the bunch was Dave Thomas who played for Burnley, QPR and Everton, gaining eight full England caps along the way. Dave was the star of the team, with his speed and skill nobody could touch him. I played against him a few times and we reminisced about those England days. Steve Bowtrell played for Leyton Orient, Pat Lowery for Newcastle and Sunderland, Alan Moody for Middlesbrough, Lyndon Hughes for West Bromwich Albion, Malcolm Webster for Arsenal and Fulham, and David Dangerfield for Swindon Town and Charlton Athletic. I will never forget those lads. As a team we were awesome and we gelled together so quickly in a matter of weeks. It's a great testimony to us that so many went on to have footballing careers.

A few weeks after my England foray I was invited to a game at Aston Villa's Villa Park. The match picked all the best lads from all of the different countries involved in schoolboy football. I went up with Dick Williamson and I had another good game. On the way back, he told me that he had been approached by six or seven scouts from clubs such as Arsenal, Spurs, Liverpool and Aston Villa who all wanted me to sign for them. I was flattered and he told me how they wanted to give me an apprenticeship, then he said, 'But you don't want to sign for them do you, there's only one club for you.' I knew what he meant, but I would have liked to have talked to these clubs although I couldn't really as I was still on Bristol City schoolboy forms. However, I had still not heard from City.

Comparing those times with today, I would probably have had an agent who would have manoeuvred me into a position where I had demanded that City release me so I could talk to other clubs, or failing that one of those clubs would have paid to bring me in. After all, I was the captain of both Bristol Boys and of England Schoolboys so in today's football I would have certainly been a hot property for clubs.

The crazy thing was that although I was having all this publicity with England, I still had no contact with Bristol City regarding playing games or any sort of regular coaching. I was their schoolboy, like many others, but there did not seem to be any sort of plan of what to do with us. Despite this I think it's important to say that there was no pressure on me at all like there would have been today. I never had family who would be in the pub telling everyone about their son who was going to be a footballer, touting me round various clubs hoping to get signed or believing everything written about me in the paper that I was going to be the next big thing. Mum, Dad and the people around me just let me get on with what I enjoyed, and that was football, but I still never thought it would be a career.

So as I had not heard anything from City I left school and sorted out an apprenticeship in painting and decorating. The family also left for a two-week holiday to Torquay, where Mum, Dad, Vernon and I stayed in a guest house. It was the start of the World Cup and Vernon was very much interested, but I wasn't bothered, which I know is strange. We watched the tournament over those two weeks and I gradually got hooked. When we got home, Vernon left for the army and I watched the games with Mum and Dad on our black and white television. I remember the final – it was a boiling hot day and the window of Garnett Street was open and nobody was about. Not everyone had a TV and those who didn't found somebody who did to watch the game with. We thought the game was won at 2-1, then a mistake I think from Jack Charlton let the Germans in to make it 2-2. We were all crushed but extra time unfolded and the rest is history. When the whistle blew we all jumped for joy as did the whole of Garnett Street. I remember watching Bobby Moore walk up those steps and thinking 'I know what that's like'; it certainly was a great day.

With the euphoria of the World Cup over, I was ready to get started on a career in painting and decorating until one night there was a knock on my door. Dad opened it and into the front room came Bristol City manager Fred Ford and scout Cliff Williams. Mum offered them tea and they explained that they wanted to sign me as an apprentice for the club and offered me £5 a week. They told me they had been monitoring my progress with Bristol Boys and England. They also had reports that the family were all City fans which they knew would help with my decision. They said it would be tough but if I worked hard then I would have a chance of making it.

We all agreed, so Fred told me to come to the club the next day to sign. With that the two men headed off, leaving the Merricks in a state of shock and euphoria. We all jumped around the room and I had never seen my parents so happy; City was our club and here I was going to sign for them. It was a dream come true for all of us. That night, it was difficult to get to sleep as I kept thinking about all the people who had helped get me there and I vowed I was not going to let them down in the next stage of my life.

3
Living the Dream

MEETING FRED Ford and Cliff Morgan in my front room was surreal to say the least. The following day I embarked on the ten-minute walk from my house to Bristol City's Ashton Gate ground, where I would be signing as an apprentice. I can honestly say I had a bit of purpose about my walk that day; after all I was on my way to possibly becoming a footballer at the club everybody I knew loved.

When I arrived at the stadium the players had just finished training and I could see them disappearing into Ashton Gate. I stood outside the main doors and saw what I presume was a member of the admin staff. He asked me what I wanted and I informed him that I was there to see manager Fred Ford, my name was Geoff Merrick and I was signing as an apprentice. He told me to follow him and we went into the corridors of the club, past pictures of former players, and I was struck by the laughter and smells of liniment coming from the dressing room as we walked by. Suddenly the man knocked on the door and a loud London accent said, 'Come in.' I was shown in and the man said,

'Fred, this is Geoff Merrick to see you.' He left, and I was alone with Fred Ford, who was dressed in nothing but a towel which was drying areas of his body that quite frankly I had no need to see. Fred never blinked an eye as he continued with his drying procedure, saying, 'All right son, how are you? I've got the forms for you here; you just need to sign them.' I also couldn't help but notice that he had only three fingers on his right hand. To this day I still don't know how Fred lost them, and I never really wanted to ask him.

He proceeded to get dressed, for which I was thankful, and we talked about what was expected of me and how pleased the club were to get my signature. I spent a couple of hours being shown round the ground and then I left for home. That evening, Mum and Dad questioned me about my signing but I thought I would leave out my first real encounter with Fred and his towel. Fred was a tough man; he had been an uncompromising wing-half for Millwall and Carlisle United in his day and Bristol City was his first venture into management. He had been in the hotseat since 1960 and had taken the club up from the Third Division but at that moment they were languishing near the bottom of the Second Division. He had, however, created a decent side and there was a good spirit among the players.

I started my apprenticeship along with Dave Prossett, who was from Hereford, Bobby Williams and Johnny Munday who were both Bristol lads, along with Ian Broomfield who I had gone to Bisham Abbey with. We also had another local lad in Graham

Tanner, I had played against Gerry Ingram who was the Wales Schoolboys captain, and there was also Nicky Burke, who was from Burnham and is somebody I have been friends with ever since. We were put in the charge of Bill Harvey, the youth team coach, who like many of the coaches around at the time was tough, funny at times, and would encourage you but if you crossed him he would come down on you like a ton of bricks. Bill had played for Grimsby Town before the war and when it ended, he decided to concentrate on coaching, although he had also managed at Luton Town and came to Ashton Gate via Swindon Town.

Our job as players was to do what we were told, listen, and to work hard, and if we did those things we just might have a chance of making it. We had games against other youth teams in cup competitions, while there was also a Bristol City team in the local suburban league, which was for players moving from youth games, then there was the A team which was playing in the Western League, followed by reserve football and then the holy grail of the first team.

I found myself mainly straight in the Western League team and it was a baptism of fire. We were coached by a guy called Alfie Rowles, another hard man who certainly whipped you into shape and you needed it as the Western League was a lonely old place if you didn't stand up for yourself. Alfie had been a star at City during the 1930s where he scored 20 goals in 24 games before a knee injury against Notts County ended his career at the age of 23. The teams in the league were the likes of Bideford and Minehead and clubs that had ex-pros in their side along with players who may have not made the grade in becoming pros themselves, so would give that extra ten per cent to knock the stuffing out of a few lads from a professional club. I remember getting a few elbows in the face along with the odd waist-high tackle but it served its purpose and toughened you up no end.

When I was not getting lumps kicked out of me in the Western League I was doing my chores as an apprentice. Bill Harvey ran a tight ship. Our day started at 9am and went on to whenever he said in the afternoon. We would sweep the terraces and clean the place up, bearing in mind that him and Fred would go through everything with a fine-toothed comb. Fred seemed to have a knack for finding dust on a high shelf somewhere. We would wash the kit with carbolic soap, clean the first team players' boots, and do some painting around the ground. Looking back we just did what we were told. I remember one of my jobs now and then was to retrieve any balls from behind the old Wills Tobacco sign at the covered end of the ground. This sign must have been about 50 feet up in the air on the top of the stand. Bill would say, 'Geoff, get up there as we need the balls for Saturday,' and I would, without hesitation, climb up the ladder and get them. It was fraught with danger as I never looked where the steel joists were, I just walked out on the steel sheeting roof without a care in the world. I was in building for 30 years after my football career and I certainly would not have asked one of my men to have gone out and done that. I can't believe how lucky I was not to get injured and can't imagine a modern academy player walking around the top of a club's stand.

Despite all of this it was the best spell of my life, and we did have some great laughs together. Chris Garland was at the club and a few years ahead of me, and although he was knocking on the first team's door he still had to knuckle down at times. We were and still are great friends though I don't remember him giving me any advice on making the grade; the only advice he ever gave me back in those days was about girls and I can't put that in this book. Chris was a real character, and I remember when we were all out on the Ashton Gate pitch working for the groundsmen, maintaining the pitch by forking it. Some of the lads had forks and some were using their feet to repair divots, which in itself was a mundane and boring job but it had to be done, especially if Fred Ford said so. Chris was having none of it and decided as he never had a fork he would just sit about and watch us. While me and Nicky Burke were forking away with our backs to the tunnel, Chris spotted Fred about to start walking down it. With that, he took the pitchfork off Nicky and started to work away on the divots, and as Fred came on to the pitch he shouted, 'Burke you lazy bastard, stop standing about and do some work like the rest of them.' We all fell about but Nicky was mortified to have felt the wrath of Fred.

But Nicky wasn't the only one who got a mouthful from Fred. Graham Tanner had a laid-back style and I recall Fred shouting, 'Tanner, put some effort into it. When I was your age I was stepping on fucking dead Germans,' and another time we all creased up laughing when we were playing a practice game and Fred shouted, 'Come on, five minutes to go,' while holding up his right hand and showing three of his fingers. That was Fred – funny sometimes when he didn't realise he was being funny.

I was progressing well and passed my driving test at 17, which was a bonus. There was a guy called Tony who lived across the road from us and he had a lovely Vauxhall Viva. Every now and then Tony let me borrow the car, especially if some of the lads were going out. He told me a friend of his in Nailsea, which was a few miles away, was selling a green Vauxhall Victor and asked if I would like to go with him to look at it. I jumped at the chance and off we went. I bought it for £75 which, considering I was on £5 a week and my mum, bless her, only asked for £1 in lodgings, was a lot of money to shell out but I had been saving. I really was living the dream – an apprentice at Bristol City and driving round with a car. The reality was the car was a bloody nightmare; it kept breaking down, and when it did go it churned out more smoke than a steam train. It caused me endless problems but the main thing was I never fell out with Tony about it, but I still have a few nightmares when any says, 'Do you remember the old Vauxhall Victor?'

I have said it before but these were great times for me, not only mixing with so many different people from different areas but making some great friends who remain so today, like Nicky Burke. Nicky was a good footballer who lived in Burnham, around 30 miles from Bristol. If we went on a night out in Bristol he would stay over at our house but we would have to share a bed. Now that's something he did not want me to put in this book, but there you go! Nicky would get a lift to the ground every day and believe it or not hitchhike home. He struggled with the money he was on as almost all of it went to his family. I remember he went and asked for a rise and was told no, so he came back to see me and said he thought he was going to give up the football as the £6.50 he was on wasn't enough. We fell about when I told him I was on £5 but he did give up his apprenticeship at City as he had to find a job with more money. He was a real loss to the game and although he stayed in part-time football, he has done really well as a successful businessman. I can't help wondering whether he would have made the grade but I'm just glad I can call him a real friend today.

Perhaps some of the great memories of those days were the first team players themselves, who were a wonderful bunch of men who I idolised. They would congregate in the Robins Café in North Street, just up from the ground. It was a real hub with smoke and laughter filling the room. The café was run by Beryl and Arthur who did the best toast ever. All the players from the first team and youth team would go there, but I was too shy to speak to some of them and at times I would wait until they were gone then go in. Beryl used to say, 'Come in love, you're part of the team,' but I was so nervous around them even though they were all fantastic to me. Players like Jack Connor, Mike Gibson, Gordon

Parr and Jantzen Derrick – all of them in some way made me a footballer. The first team would play on the car park at Ashton Gate and if they were short, Fred would shout, 'Geoff, get a bib on,' and I would join them.

Jantzen was incredible with the ball and there was nobody to touch him in terms of skill. He was a real talent. Jack Connor was another player who talked me through games, particularly when I made the reserves. Jack would give me advice before, during and after games, which was so valuable to me.

Jack Boxley was another one who gave advice and showed an interest in my development. Jack had been a great outside-half for City during the 1950s and he was now retired and running a car sales garage just across the road from Ashton Gate. He sold me an old Humber Sceptre, which was lovely but it was blue and white. I'm sure that's why he sold it as it was in Bristol Rovers' colours. Looking back, I must have been really desperate to get rid of the Vauxhall Victor to drive round south Bristol in a blue and white car.

On the field the club were languishing in the Second Division when Fred Ford was sacked by chairman Harry Dolman. Harry was a larger-than-life character who loved Bristol City. He made his money in engineering and he had a lot of time for the youngsters at the club. Harry was the man who arranged for me to meet and have my photo taken with City's legendary ex-England centre-forward John Atyeo when I signed as an apprentice. Harry said the reason for the sacking was that Fred didn't spend any money. The players were so heartbroken at Fred's departure that a group of them went to Harry's home in the Chew Valley to ask him to reconsider, but their appeals fell upon deaf ears.

I was gutted at the loss of Fred, who incidentally ended up across the other side of Bristol at Rovers. He gave me my start in the game and he was always supportive towards my career, even coming to games in later life when I was captaining Bristol City through the First Division years. We always had a chat and he always told me if I had played well or I had not. It's a very strange atmosphere at a football club when a manager leaves and this was my first taste of it, whereas for the more established players you could see they were all worried as we all know the game is about opinions and many knew that if the manager did not like you then you would be moved on. I was just as worried; after all my nature is one of worrying over things so I really needed this like a hole in the head.

At this point I was around the first team squad on a regular basis, going away with them to games and although not playing I was learning from them and being in and around the dressing room. We also socialised as a unit and I was very much part of it. I remember a particular night when Jack Connor was asked to go to Burnham Town Hall to judge a 'personality competition'. Girls would parade in swimwear and Jack would compare their personality based on who had the biggest boobs. Well we were not going to miss a trip like that so off we went to support Jack. After the event, we went on to a party along with the contestants at the Pontins Leisure Park in Brean, which was just up the road. I was 17 and I saw the girl who had won, with her mate, who was at the time being chatted up by a few City lads. I was new to all this but eventually her mate came over to me and introduced herself as Wendy. It was at that moment I fell in love and I will go into more detail about my wonderful wife Wendy later in the book.

The uncertainty at City was ended when Alan Dicks walked through the doors. He was young, confident, well dressed with a bit of a sun tan and a million miles away from Fred Ford. This was Alan's first job as a manager. Alan had played as a full-back for Chelsea and Southend United and had also been assistant manager at Coventry City under Jimmy Hill. He introduced himself and his number two, John Sillett, and told us that he wanted to achieve promotion. When he left that meeting there were a few grumbles from the players that he was no Fred Ford but he did mention youth and I was happy with that. I remember Alan's first coaching session which introduced thinking about the game and trying to think of the next pass rather than training sessions of just running and running. Some of the older pros had a field day taking the piss out of his methods but in hindsight I realise Alan had to stamp his authority on that dressing room and players like me were the future whereas there were a few he thought were the past.

My career seemed to take off as I was awarded a contract by Alan and given a £20 wage. It was also heartbreaking to see some of the lads I had done my apprenticeship with on the ground staff being let go. Alan, like Fred, saw something in me and included me in first team training and the odd away trip. If I'm honest, I knew I wasn't that far away from the first team. At home, Mum and Dad were worried about the upheaval at the club and how it may affect me but our main cause of concern was that Mum was ill in hospital. I visited her every day and I will always remember one day after a visit I walked along the hospital corridor and saw a man pushing a trolley with a few local papers on, so I asked if I could buy one. He said to take it. I continued to read it as I walked along and there was another Merrick headline: 'MERRICK STARTS AGAINST ASTON VILLA'. Yes, once again I found out my fate from the back pages of the local paper. I rolled it up and went back to see Mum to show her, and although she was poorly she was thrilled and said, 'Your dad will be made up,' which he was when I got home.

So I was picked for my debut away at Aston Villa along with goalkeeper Barry Watling, who had been a youth player at Leyton Orient and came into the side as Mike Gibson was injured. It was the penultimate game of the season and we had stayed up, while Villa were mid-table, so I think Alan thought it would be a good time to blood some youth in the side. Going up on the coach, I was just concentrating on not making any mistakes and the lads were brilliant with me, joking around as they always did and making me fee relaxed.

Villa Park is a massive and imposing ground. I had played there as a kid but that was nothing like being in front of around 15,000 screaming Villa fans. The team that day was Watling,

Jacobs, Briggs, Wimshurst, Connor, Merrick, Derrick, Crowe, Garland, Quigley, Bartley, Bush (sub). Jack Connor settled me down and I remember Villa had a big centre-forward called Brian Greenhalgh, who was a seasoned pro and as we went up for the ball he smashed me into the ground. I knew then that this was pro football. Jack came over and told me to leave Greenhalgh to him and for me to not go diving in and back off at times.

Villa went 1-0 up then Jantzen Derrick pulled one back before they made it 2-1. We came back at them with a goal from Chris Crowe to make it 2-2, and with only about half an hour gone Chris Garland produced a bit of magic to make it 3-2 before we sealed the win in the second half with a goal from Terry Bush. As the whistle blew, I was shattered, black and blue and splattered with mud. It was our first win at Villa Park in 19 attempts. Personally I was elated that I had stood up to the rigours of professional football and come through the experience. I thought of how those Western League games at such a young age had helped me, and even Brian Greenhalgh came over and shook my hand, telling me what a good game I had given him. I just nodded as I don't think I had the strength to speak. Alan Dicks told me I had done well as did the rest of the lads. So that was it, I had started my journey as a footballer. Or had I?

4

Is it the End?

AFTER MY display against Aston Villa I was rested for the last game of the season, away at Middlesbrough. As far as Alan Dicks and his staff were concerned I would be okay in the first team, and even more important than that was that the players I was around thought the same. They knew I was young and a bit wet behind the ears but I had given everything at Villa Park and I believe I had their respect, which was important to me.

While the players went off for the summer, many away with their families to different holiday spots dotted around home and Europe, I spent the close-season working on the farm and I would not have wanted to be anywhere else. I loved the open countryside and the clean air; it was a million miles away from football and all its pressures and I knew very early in my career that I never wanted to lose this part of my life no matter how high I climbed as a player.

Bristol City were more than happy for me to work there as they knew I would come back to them as fit as when I had left at the end of the season.

I was now seeing Wendy, who I had met at the beauty pageant in Burnham. Wendy was from Burnham and was a hairdresser. During my free time we would go off for the day and flit between Burnham and Bristol. Wendy loved Bristol and sometimes she would stay over at Mum and Dad's when we would have a night out, in separate beds I have to make clear as Mum would have had none of that funny stuff going on under her roof. It wasn't for the lack of trying on my part though.

During pre-season I would occasionally think about the new campaign and what it would bring. This was going to be the first real campaign in charge for Alan Dicks and his backroom staff so I knew we all had to impress to make sure we were in his plans. When we all came back from the summer there was the usual banter as some of the lads had put on a few pounds. Alan's assistant John Sillett worked us hard though. John had played with Alan at Chelsea and he was certainly an imposing man who looked like a Royal Marine with his crew-cut hair and loud booming voice to match.

The main addition to the squad, along with a few youth lads who had been promoted, was midfielder Bobby Kellard from Portsmouth. Bobby was a great player, tough and determined, and great with the ball. He was incredibly popular with the fans and the lads, and we called him 'Dud' as he looked like the actor and comedian Dudley Moore. We started the 1968/69 campaign with a 1-0 home defeat at the hands of Fulham. I was named as substitute and did not get on but I got my home debut in the following game, against Sheffield United. The team was pretty much the same as my debut except for Bobby and Mike Gibson, who had returned in goal for us. I would like to say I was not nervous but as you probably know by now that is my nature. I just did not want to let anybody down, whether it was my team-mates or the fans.

I recall in the build-up the papers writing about my forthcoming tussle with winger Alan Woodward, who became a legend at Sheffield United over the years. Alan was quick and very skilful and you did not have to be a genius to know that he was probably relishing a game against a young lad making his home debut. There were 20,000 packed into Ashton Gate and among them were my family and friends ready to cheer me on. Looking back, I remember Woodward getting the better of me on a few occasions but I think I pulled his shirt at one point and swung him round on to his backside which must have startled him. We went a goal down in the second half but I managed to get down to the byline and put a cross in for our centre-forward John Galley to smash home to make it 1-1.

It was an incredible feeling as all the lads came over to congratulate me. I think John was more pleased with my cross than he was with the goal he had just scored. I think nowadays that would be called an assist and there would be various graphs and calculations on how many assists I had made, but back then it was just a cross. The crowd were superb and they cheered my every move. I have to say that's how Bristol City fans have always been, they have always encouraged a local lad, and they certainly did for me that day.

The game ended 1-1 and I had the papers telling me that I was the best defender on the pitch. All of that sort of stuff went over my head as I was only interested in what I had done for the team and the fans. Alan Dicks praised my performance and as far as I was concerned it was on to the next game, Bolton Wanderers at home. As they had done before, the local press picked out the battle I would be facing – this time it was Bolton's new £65,000 signing from Wolverhampton Wanderers, Terry Wharton. Terry was a quick and skilful player, much like winger Gordon Taylor who I would also be up against. This would not be the last time that I crossed paths with Taylor.

Much was also made in the press of the fact that I was 17 years old and my full-back partner was Trevor Jacobs, who was 21. I believe it was the youngest pairing in the Second Division and reporters felt at the time we may be vulnerable when facing experience, but we all thought this was the only way we were going to learn. The team also reflected the fact that Alan Dicks was starting to put his faith in youth as he was giving us the chance.

The game against Bolton was on a Tuesday night under floodlights, which was magical at Ashton Gate. There is nothing like playing under lights; I don't know what it is but there's something about it that gives you goosebumps. I felt the same when I would go to matches when I was a kid. The game was fast and competitive, and the 20,000 fans in the ground made it seem double that with the noise they produced. Chris Garland put us 1-0 up then Terry Wharton pulled one back with a piece of skill that showed why he was worth the money Bolton had paid for him. We went in level and things were going fine, although Alan was annoyed we had let them back in it. As the second half started our confidence grew as we got more and more of the ball. In the 53rd minute there was a scramble in our box and I remember the Bolton captain Gareth Williams came crashing in for the ball. As he caught me I went over on my right leg and jarred it sideways. I went down immediately and was seen to by club physio Les Bardsley. Les worked on it and I was in agony, although I told him I would be fine.

Les left the field and watched me from the sidelines as I crashed to the ground again after standing on my leg. The game was stopped and I was helped off by Les and a member of the St John Ambulance team. Once in the dressing room the club doctor looked at my injury and he and Les decided I had damaged my medial knee ligaments, which was dreadful news. I can't say I was distraught as I did not realise the seriousness of the problem. I was sent to the Chesterfield Hospital in the Clifton area of Bristol where I had an operation and was there for two weeks. The lads visited, as did my family and Wendy. They were all cheerful but I know in the back of everyone's mind was whether I would get back to play again. As far as I was concerned, I believed I would, but you must bear in mind these were the early stages of what could turn out to be a long process.

After hospital I was sent home with instructions to stay in bed for a week before coming to the club every day to work with Les. Being injured is terrible for a player at any time, but even more so when your established fans miss you as they know what you can bring to a team. When it happens while you are a youngster just starting out, you have barely been able to show what you can do and that makes it all the more frustrating. I had those feelings, although the diehard City fans, of which there were many, knew what I was all about due to my appearances in the reserves. At the time, reserve games were at Ashton Gate and would get crowds of more than 2,000 along with good coverage in the local newspaper.

It was a long process of recovery which was not only physically tough with some exhausting exercises but mentally tough, especially when you would see the first team together as they prepared for training and games while I was on my own with Les. It also didn't help that the club were informed that myself and Ian Broomfield, who was also injured at the time, were called up for a three-day England youth trial at Lilleshall. We were both unable to attend and my chance to try and get another international cap was gone.

Despite the gloom regarding my injury, the lads were great and supportive with plenty of encouragement but there was no substitute for being in among them and playing. After a few months I was up and about and running but it was always a little tentative as I wasn't sure that my knee could stand up to the full rigours of a game. With this in mind, I was on my own running around the cinder track that went around the Ashton Gate pitch when I decided I really needed to give it a full-blown test. It really was shit or bust, so I went for it and sprinted down the touchline then all of a sudden the knee locked and I appeared to fly through the air before I came crashing to the ground with a massive thud.

I lay there for a bit and knew that something was plainly not right. I got up and due to the cinder track I was full of cuts and bruises, not to mention the fact that I could hardly walk. I struggled to move but I managed to get to the medical room where I saw Les and I told him what had happened. He could see that I was in a real state and typical of Les, he looked at it and said, 'It's the cartilage, so at least we know what we're dealing with.' I was in real pain as it appeared my knee had locked as the cartilage had moved. This meant a further lay-off, which was difficult to take. Today the cartilage would be done by keyhole surgery and the player would be back after a few weeks but for me it was another op and loads more rehab. I really was at the end of my tether as I thought this could be the end for me.

The process was long, around ten weeks, but I kept myself busy. I remember being up and about in Bedminster and seeing my old mate Rob Summerhill, who was a diehard City fan. We were both collecting the sports paper from the newsagent and he asked how I was and tentatively said that the paper had rumours that I was finished. He didn't mean any malice and was genuinely concerned for me, but I remember saying, 'Oh, do they? We will see about that.' I think hearing that from somebody I knew really spurred me on to work even harder to get back, which I certainly did.

In total, it was almost 12 months on from the injury against Bolton that I returned in a reserve game at Ashton Gate against Plymouth Argyle. Everyone at the club was pleased to see me back, as were the fans and my family, but they were not as pleased as me. My only concern was how I would fare in my first tackle and my first sprint. The answer was there was no problem – the knee passed with flying colours as we won 3-2.

It was such a relief and after a few more reserve appearances, Alan Dicks picked me for a home League Cup tie against Exeter City. I was over the moon to be back in the throes of competitive football and especially at Ashton Gate. I was not only pleased that Alan and his staff had shown faith in me but the Exeter game was the first match Wendy had ever attended. She told me later that she stood in the old covered end of the ground and the policemen were really kind as they got her a box to stand on so she could see what was happening on the pitch. I suppose that was the level of hospitality for wives and girlfriends back in the day.

We won 3-2 and my match fitness was certainly coming back. I particularly enjoyed playing in the back four with Brian Drysdale, Trevor Jacobs and captain Dickie Rooks. I felt we had a really good understanding among us which could only be good for the future. Alan then kept more or less the same team for the home game with our Severnside rivals Cardiff City. I remember ex Bristol City player Brian Clark and a young John Toshack really testing not only me but the whole of the back four as Cardiff won 2-0. I was disappointed, as we all were, but I was pleased that my knee had certainly been put to the test by the Cardiff forwards.

Three days later I faced Sheffield United at Bramall Lane. The game certainly started with a bang as Jack Connor scored an own goal to put them 1-0 up then they made it 2-0 before Trevor Tainton pulled one back for us with 20 minutes on the clock. During the game I was having a real tussle with the Sheffield United midfielder Len Badger. Len was a short powerhouse of a player, really strong and quick, and we were at each other right from the off. Then, with around 30 minutes gone, we went in for a challenge and to this day I don't know how it happened but he seemed to flick me over his head and as I came towards the ground I put out an arm and felt a terrible pain shoot through my body. As I lay there in a heap it was plain to everybody that something was wrong. I was carried off and taken down the tunnel where the Sheffield United club doctor was waiting along with Les. They immediately agreed that I had dislocated my left elbow. I really could not believe it. The doctor said that he could pop it into place right there but I said 'no chance' so off I went to the hospital.

I was accompanied by City director Lionel Smart, who sat with me for what seemed an age before I was seen to. The lads lost 2-1 and they were staying in Sheffield as they had a game against Huddersfield Town in a few days' time. My arm was put back in place but I was still in agony as I was dispatched back to Bristol on the overnight sleeper train complete with my arm in a sling. The sleeper certainly did not live up to its title as I lay in my compartment thinking about how long this lay-off would be while being buffeted with the carriage bumping up and down every five minutes. It also seemed to stop at every town from Sheffield to Bristol and I eventually arrived home at 7am the following day.

Just as I was starting to come back after a few months off, I was training and slowly getting back into the first team so I could see a real light at the end of the tunnel. Alan used to mix training up and take us to various places just for a change of scenery. One particular session was down in Weston-super-Mare. I went to tackle team-mate Peter Spiring and he just brushed past me. As he did I fell and would you believe it I dislocated my right elbow. You really could not make it up, and again I was out for months.

My injury run was incredibly difficult to deal with. During my first real full season, 1969/70, I had managed three games, and in 1970/71 – although after the injuries I was in and out of the side – I had still only made 13 appearances. I had been battling injuries for around two and a half years and really couldn't seem to get a regular place in the team. To be fair to Alan Dicks, he encouraged me and he knew when I was fit I was as good as any defender at the club but again I was frustrated that I was not able to establish myself in the team that he was building. I knew that although Alan had been supportive, I really needed to establish myself in the side and get myself ready for the start of the new season.

As the end of that campaign approached, it really helped that I was included in a short tour of Spain where we were going to play a few games. Alan was very keen for us to go, mainly I think for us to bond at the end of a tough season where the club had finished fourth from bottom in the Second Division and avoided relegation by four points, but also another reason for the tour was to top up his tan. It was a great trip for me in terms of getting ready for the next season and we played two games in our tour of the Costa Brava. First up was a 3-1 defeat to Espanyol in front of 35,000 fans, including a lot of English supporters who were on holiday cheering us on. It was a great experience and it was incredibly uplifting for me to be back on a pitch playing with the lads. Well, I say pitch, it really was as hard as the Ashton Gate car park but it didn't matter as I was playing again. To be out running, tackling and heading without worrying about getting injured was a brilliant feeling. I came through that game, much to the delight of Alan and his backroom staff who were clearly thrilled at my progress.

During the trip we got the chance to have a look around Barcelona's Camp Nou stadium. It was incredible and looked like a spaceship on the outskirts of the city. The pitch seemed small and the seating seemed to rise up through the sky forever. I would certainly have loved to have played there with a full house. What was amusing, particularly after what I had been through, was that they showed us the medical facilities which included a small hospital and operating theatre in the bowels of the stadium. I got a bit of stick about how I would have loved it there, as did Les, who a lot of the lads ribbed about not knowing what the machines were for and where he would keep his bucket and sponge.

The second game was a win against Calella, who I think were in the Spanish third division. We won 2-1 again in front of a crowd made up of British holidaymakers and although it was only two games against mediocre opposition there was a real buzz about us. *Evening Post* journalist Peter Godsiff, who was a wonderful man, came out with us and his reports about my displays were glowing. He interviewed Alan who said I had been the star of the tour. By now you know that bigging myself up is not my style but this showed how hard I had worked to get back and even though those games were on hard, bobbly pitches, the way I felt after it might as well have been Wembley.

We returned to Bristol after a few days and I was back on the farm and ready for the next season. When 1971/72 arrived you could sense as a squad we were ready. Our first game was at home to Millwall in front of a packed Ashton Gate. My debut against Villa seemed now a million miles away. Alan Dicks and his chief scout Tony Collins, who was a legend at spotting talent, had slowly removed some players and brought new faces in, gradually shaping the squad into what Alan wanted. It was sad to see the likes of Jantzen Derrick, Jack Connor, Alec Briggs and Bobby Kellard go. In return, Alan had promoted from the youth team and made some fantastic buys.

From the youth team came Ray Cashley in goal. Ray had some massive shoes to fill in the shape of Mike Gibson, who was now his backup. It is testimony to Mike that he encouraged and worked with Ray even though he was going to be filling his shoes and in time Ray proved to be a worthy replacement for Mike – not bad for a lad who started his career as a full-back. I have mentioned the great signing that was Brian Drysdale from Hartlepool a few seasons before. He could and would run all day long. Trevor Tainton had come into his own in midfield and again he was a product of the youth team, as were Peter Spiring and forward Keith Fear, who was a top-class goalscorer. The youngster who filled the boots of Bobby Kellard, sold to Leicester City, was called Gerry Gow. Many in the media and also some fans thought he wouldn't be up to the job but they plainly didn't know Gerry. He was a class footballer who gave nothing but 100 per cent and expected the same from those around him.

Personality-wise we could not have been more different. Gerry was loud on the pitch and very vocal but I was more quiet. He was a major force in our future success. Gerry had bags of confidence and I couldn't help noticing that there was an air of belief about all the youth team lads, not in a disparaging and cocky way but in a way that when called upon they did their job and knew they could do it. I certainly never had the confidence they had at that period in my footballing career.

Another great signing was Gerry Sweeney. Gerry could play anywhere, was the joker in the team and the one who always finished first in the cross-country runs in training. He was originally at Celtic under the great Jock Stein and although his progress at the Glasgow giants was limited, he had found his way to Ashton Gate via Morton for the princely sum of £22,000, which was incredible business on City's part. Sweeney made his debut that August day against Millwall with a lad called John Emanuel. John was from Wales and had slipped through the net before coming to us from Welsh non-league club Ferndale.

Unbelievably for the first game in August, the match nearly got postponed due to a waterlogged pitch. There had been a massive downpour and the pitch was flooded but the groundsman Mike Lillington worked wonders to get the game on. It would have been a massive anti-climax for all of us who were raring to go if he hadn't worked so hard. The Millwall match was an explosive start to the season as we drew 3-3 with Gerry Gow, Gerry Sweeney and Chris Garland getting on the scoresheet. I had had a real tough game against striker Derek Possee, who scored one of the Millwall goals, and it really was a return to the blood and guts of Second Division football.

We started the season well and in our first seven games we had only lost once so we found ourselves sat near the top of the table. It was a shock during our run that my mate Chris Garland was sold to Chelsea in the September for £100,000, which was a lot of money, but it was a move that Chris wanted so we wished him well. I have to admit I could not understand why anybody would want to leave the club, even for more money and the bright lights of London's King's Road. I guess I was just consumed by Bristol City. It was all I ever really wanted.

We knew Chris would be a loss but our initial form meant we were buzzing as a squad until a 1-0 home defeat to high-flyers

Norwich City brought us back to earth. It was certainly pivotal for me as I had made a bad clearance which let Norwich player Dave Stringer smash the ball in for the winning goal.

Incidents like that played on my mind. I turned things over in my head. What if I had done this? Could I have done that? All of it just went round and round. I wasn't the type of player to think 'oh well, on to the next game'; I would be like a bear with a sore head for days if we lost. I really took it personally and thought I had let the fans down. So when Alan Dicks called me over to him at the training ground before a match against Blackpool I feared that I could be dropped.

We spoke and he asked me if I would be captain. To be honest I was in a state of shock; the captaincy had been moving between Ken Wimshurst and Dickie Rooks who were both top professionals and very experienced in the game. Alan just said he thought it would suit me down to the ground. I accepted and was so proud that I was going to captain my club, it was the ultimate accolade for me, although the anxiety kicked in when I thought about how the players would react, especially the older ones. I worried how the senior pros would take to being led by a young lad of 20, but my fears fell away when to a man the first team squad all thought it was a good idea. The press also picked up on the fact that I was the youngest captain in all of the four divisions and they were really positive regarding my appointment, which helped with my confidence.

We beat Blackpool 4-0 in my first game as captain and I got a great reception from the fans. It was a big responsibility for me, and although I worried about it at first I have to say I enjoyed it. My role wasn't just on the pitch and I was also invited, sometimes along with Wendy, to represent the club at various functions. I struggled at first, particularly if I had to make a speech, but I think I really grew into the position both on and off the pitch. My style on the pitch was not one of shouting and bawling players out but trying to give advice and encouragement, and it seemed to work. I was also aware of the responsibility towards all the lads at the club, like the youth team. I remember how shy I was when I was around the first-teamers so I always made time for any of the youth team if they wanted a chat or just some words of encouragement in training. I just wanted to treat them as I would have liked to have been treated.

I celebrated the last game of the season with a 4-2 win at home against Oxford United. I say celebrated as it was also my 21st birthday. The season had been a mixed affair and at one point it looked as though we could have had a chance at promotion, but we fell away and finished eighth, which considering the previous season's performance was a massive improvement. Everybody was happy with the final placing, including the fans, as it looked like we were building something together.

After all the games were over we had the supporters' club evening dinner at a hotel in central Bristol. It was where they would be announcing the player of the year, voted by the supporters. It was a big black tie affair and it gave us a chance to meet fans and sponsors. The evening was great and it got better when City midfielder Gerry Sharpe, who had been player of the year for the previous season, read out the result of the poll. In fourth place with four per cent of the votes Ray Cashley; third with six per cent was John Emanuel; second with 17 per cent was John Galley; and then he announced that I was the winner with 65 per cent. The room exploded with applause and for a moment I was dumbstruck. I weaved my way through the tables still with the applause of the supporters and team-mates ringing in my ears to collect my award. It was a fabulous moment for me. I had won the award all the players coveted and become captain in a season where myself and Brian Drysdale had not missed a game, which when compared to my previous years with injury was incredible.

A few weeks after the season had ended the club were going on a tour of Iran, organised by Tony Collins. Tony had a contact in Tehran who coached one of the teams out there. The lads were all looking forward to it as it was a mysterious part of the world. But there would be no exotic trip for this Bedminster lad as I had a meeting with Wendy Ashton on 27 May at Bristol Registry Office for our wedding ceremony. Life certainly could not get any better.

5

Cup Glory

WENDY AND I were married at Bristol Registry Office on 27 May 1972. My best man was my brother Vernon and it was a wonderful day. All of our family were there, along with a smattering of friends and players from the club. Chris Garland came along with his wife Trish. You could tell Chris was in the big league at Chelsea as he had just returned from an end-of-season tour of Barbados with the club, whereas me and Wendy were looking forward to a honeymoon in Bournemouth. It really did make us laugh.

Another guest was my former back-four partner Jack Connor, who was coaching at Everton. Jack did not come to the service as he got lost but he made it to the reception at the Blue Bowl inn in Chew Magna, on the outskirts of the city. Jack always found his way to the pub. We knew the landlord at the Blue Bowl as we would go drinking there, and they did a great job in laying the event on for us.

Our honeymoon was great. It was wonderful to be away from football and just spend time together. Myself and Wendy had also bought a lovely three-bedroomed house in a quiet place called Backwell, some ten miles from Bristol. The house was in the countryside, which ticked a box for me regarding my farming dreams. Although I couldn't have the cows and chickens I longed for in the garden, it was still a place where I felt very much at home. We paid £5,000 for it and I had to take a mortgage out on it as I was only on £100 a week, so club chairman Robert Hobbs – who had taken over from Harry Dolman after the latter became president – had to be my guarantor.

Things were certainly moving fast for us as a couple and I was also involved in many things off the field as captain, which I really enjoyed. The local paper, the *Bristol Evening Post*, asked if I would write a weekly column for them. I was paid £25 for each column and I wrote them all myself, with Wendy checking and dictating my words over the phone to the paper to publish. We really were thrown into the limelight a bit as people seemed to be interested in us. Wendy just took it all in her stride although she never really had any interest in football and neither did her family, so she just thought it was the norm.

I also found myself on the cover of the club programme that season, immortalised in a drawing of me holding a ball and leading the team out. It really was a bit surreal and later on in the year I was invited to the *Evening Post* Sports Personality of the Year awards at the Grand Hotel in Bristol. It was a really glittering affair with sports stars such as England and Somerset cricketer Brian Close, England and Bristol rugby player John

Pullin, Olympic weightlifter Precious McKenzie and a host of other local sport stars. I came second in the voting, which had been done by the readers of the *Post*. The winner was Bristol Rovers goalkeeper Dickie Shepherd, who had performed heroics in a penalty shoot-out against Sheffield United as Rovers won the Watney Cup that year. Dickie was a lovely bloke and I was as pleased for him as I was that I never had to make a speech.

All of this was great but it would have been pointless if I did not also do the business on the field, which was what was really important. Alan Dicks was still perfecting his squad as players came and went. In that season John Galley left for Nottingham Forest and was a big loss to the team. John was a great pro whose goals had certainly kept us in the division. Also leaving was my old partner Dickie Rooks, along with Ken Wimshurst, who went on to the coaching staff at the club. Alan brought in the experienced Bobby Gould up front, and also moved in players from the youth team such as Tom Ritchie, Gary Collier and Dave Rodgers, who were all talented.

The only other signing was Donnie Gillies, who arrived from Morton for £30,000 midway through the season, just like Bobby. Donnie was another funny guy who joined the Scottish mafia at the club, which at the time included Gerry Sweeney, Gerry Gow and Tom Ritchie. These four were hilarious and made the dressing room tick. They also added a bit of spice to the five-a-side games in training as they became England v Scotland with nobody taking any prisoners. Sometimes those matches became so competitive that Alan would have to call a halt to them. But there was no nastiness, we were just mates together – that was the spirit we had. We may not have been the best footballers in the league but we had a fantastic spirit which carried us through at times.

One of my lasting memories of that season was when we were drawn against West Ham United in the League Cup at Upton Park. For me it was a dream come true as I would be sharing a pitch with my idol Bobby Moore. I can't tell you how thrilling it was to go up for the toss with me shaking hands with one of the greatest players ever. He was my idol right from that day where I watched him lift the World Cup on our old TV as a kid in Garnett Street. Bobby was a real role model with his timing and tackling second to none. He did not have a lot of pace but he didn't need it as he read the game so well. In an era where a lot of defenders would cut you in half, he just moved forwards away from danger by steering opposition players where he wanted them to go. Bobby made tackling an art and I learnt so much from watching him. I really aspired to be like him.

In that game at Upton Park, he was his usual classy self as they beat us 2-1, but I will never forget being on the same pitch as him. Later in my career I met Bobby many times and spent time in his company. He asked about me and my career and I was bowled over that he knew who I was, but that was him all over – always interested in other people. You would never have thought that he was one of the best players ever to play the game as he was so humble and unassuming. Being in his company is still one of the great thrills of my career.

Our season gave us a glimpse of what we could achieve as we finished fifth but in reality we were always playing catch-up to the likes of Burnley and QPR, who went up to the First Division. The positive angle to the season was that we had improved our league position and the lads were becoming a strong and difficult team to play against. I had played 42 games and was injury free, which again was a bonus. The talk all through the summer of 1973 was whether I was for sale. There were inquiries from Liverpool, Coventry City, Everton and Nottingham Forest about me, and Alan Dicks and the board went on record as saying that if I did go it would be for something nearer £150,000 rather than the £100,000 that was being put on the table. My own thoughts were that I was flattered that these clubs were interested in buying me; it was a vindication that I was playing well, and that was a massive boost to my confidence.

I was also being pushed by some in the media for an England under-23 call-up, although I did laugh when England manager Alf Ramsey was asked by the press whether Merrick was in his plans and he replied that I was injured. They informed him that I wasn't and he said, 'I thought Alan Merrick was injured.' It appeared he had got me mixed up with a West Bromwich Albion defender, so in hindsight perhaps a call-up was a bit further away than I thought.

I didn't find all the transfer talk unsettling as although these were all great teams, I had no wish whatsoever to leave my beloved

Bristol City no matter how much I was being offered. But it was never an option for me – I honestly thought that I could achieve my goals, which were to get to the top flight and play for England with my hometown club. I can't really emphasise enough how important staying with City was. To put it all into context a lot of the clubs were offering more money than I was on along with signing-on fees that certainly would have paid off my house in Backwell, but I really tried to put all of it to the back of my mind.

At the end of the season I missed out on another tour as the lads set off for the USA for a couple of matches. I would be lying if I said I didn't fancy going but I had other things on my mind, such as the imminent birth of our daughter Charlotte, or Charlie as she has always been known. I remember when Wendy told me she was expecting. I had a beautiful Ford Escort Sport which was another purchase from Jack Boxley. It really was the dog's bollocks as they say, and I loved it. I picked Wendy up from her place of work in Bristol and we proceeded to drive home. It was on that journey to Backwell that she told me she was pregnant and I nearly crashed the bloody car as I was so shocked. I also remember saying, 'Pregnant, bloody hell, I've only just bought this car, I hope that doesn't have to go.' In case you're wondering, the car stayed and my beautiful daughter was born some months later, making us a real family.

On the field, despite all the transfer talk I got down to the business of trying to get the Robins to improve on our previous finish of fifth. We started the 1973/74 season in great form, losing once in an eight-game run but towards the end of the year inconsistency kicked in and the pressure started to mount on Alan Dicks as we went from being one of the front-runners in the league to finding ourselves sliding towards the bottom half.

A real release for us was the FA Cup. We drew 1-1 at home to Hull City in the third round, where I managed to get on the scoresheet with a diving header, then won the replay 1-0 through a Trevor Tainton goal and found ourselves drawn against Hereford United. For the Hereford game, Alan decided to take us away for a few days to a tiny place called How Caple in Herefordshire. It was a large, gothic-type stately home with grounds and not really much else to distract us. We trained on a patch of grass but not before we removed the ducks and chickens, so you really had to be careful if you fancied a sliding tackle as you would be covered from head to toe in chicken shit. All of this added to the fun we had and there was also a ghost sighting by the young Howard Pritchard, who came running down the stairs of the house with his hair all stuck up adamant that he had seen a spectre in his room. We were just pissing ourselves laughing at the state of him. I also had a bit of a panic before the game as I had left my jock strap at home and I had to get Wendy to send it to me as quick as possible, much to the hilarity of the lads, but to her credit it arrived on time.

The pitch at Hereford's Edgar Street was just as bad as the stately home grounds; it was an allotment of a pitch and with driving rain and a hurricane of a wind we really didn't fancy it against our Third Division hosts. I remember Ernie Hunt was fantastic that day. Ernie had initially arrived from Coventry City on loan but ended up with us for a season. He was a great footballer who always had an eye for goal and he was a great bloke, really funny at times and a perfect addition to the team, so it was a shame he didn't stay for long. That afternoon at Edgar Street though, he was brilliant, causing Hereford all sorts of problems. We won the game 1-0 and yours truly got another goal with another header. As we trudged off the pitch we were all so covered in mud that it was hard to distinguish who was in your team and who was not.

We stayed the night in How Caple and in the morning we drove home, stopping for lunch at Tintern Abbey. We had the radio on while travelling so we could listen to the draw for the fifth round. We came out with a home tie so we all said 'that will do', then out came Leeds United who were at the time probably the biggest team in Europe. They certainly were the biggest in the UK. We couldn't believe it and we jumped about and the stationary coach was rocking from side to side as we celebrated what we knew would be a fantastic game for the red half of Bristol.

Almost immediately the press went into overdrive as did the fans, and there was a clamour for tickets as queues went round the block at Ashton Gate when they came on sale. The local TV reporters wanted to interview us all and asked us how we felt about playing a team of internationals who were unbeaten in something like 40 games and the previous season had appeared in the FA Cup Final as well as the European Cup Winners' Cup Final. What could I say when I was asked if I thought we could beat them? To be honest, I was terrified we were going to get a hiding and I was never going to come out and say we could win as I didn't want to upset Leeds and have my quotes pinned on their dressing room wall. It wasn't my way anyway to make bold statements. Local sports presenter Roger Malone always used to say to me that I should be bolder in my predictions and statements but I was just happy to be respectful and see what happened on the pitch.

During all this media hype we were still not pulling up any trees in the league with defeats against Sheffield Wednesday and Bolton Wanderers as we were heading towards the bottom half of the table, but the fans were caught up in FA Cup fever as the big day approached. Alan Dicks was certainly a man who believed in superstitions so he packed us off to How Caple again for a few days before the tie as he wanted things to be just like the run-up to the Hereford United game. The stay was great but Howard never saw his ghost, although Wendy did send me a G-string in the post to replicate me forgetting the jock strap, so I came down to dinner with it on my head which made the lads fall about laughing. When we came back to Bristol it was full-on for the game. We did countless press and TV interviews and we were all happy when the Saturday afternoon arrived, if I'm honest.

I have always loved the FA Cup and I must say I hate the way it had been devalued now with teams resting players and not really making it a priority. It's the greatest cup competition in the world and it gave us City players the chance to line up against a great team, and what a team it was that cold February afternoon at a packed-out Ashton Gate: Harvey, Yorath, Cherry, Bremner, McQueen, Hunter, Lorimer, Jordan, Jones, Giles, Madeley. Nobody rested, just as an FA Cup team should be. We went with Cashley, Sweeney, Drysdale, Gow, Collier, Merrick, Tainton, Ritchie, Fear, Gillies, Hunt. It was a great side, seven of whom had come through the youth ranks at the club. Nobody gave us a prayer, and I could see why because Leeds were better players than us, but what we did have was determination and we were not only team-mates, we were friends who would run through a brick wall for each other.

When I walked up to the centre circle to shake Billy Bremner's hand the whole of Ashton Gate was rocking. The atmosphere was incredible. The game was, as predicted, a tight affair at first and we had a few chances, as did they. They certainly came at us hoping to bully us out of the game but the lads, particularly Gerry Gow, were phenomenal in dealing with these top players. We went 1-0 down through Bremner minutes before half-time and it was a blow as we were in my opinion the better team, but later in the second half Keith Fear made it 1-1 and Ashton Gate erupted. We kept pressing them and I really thought we were going to get another. As the game ended 1-1 with a replay to look forward to, I thought we were the better side but many thought we had even less of a chance up at Elland Road. However, we really believed that we had nothing to fear and all the emphasis was now on Leeds to finish us off.

The aftermath of the draw was that we were all over the national newspapers as they all reported how Bristol City had held the mighty Leeds United and could have beaten them. I think it got to some of the Leeds players as after the game they left the dressing room and went straight to the coach instead of having a drink in the players' bar. We watched ourselves on *Match of the Day* that evening and I was really pleased for the fans and in particular all the people who worked at Ashton Gate on matchdays to see their side in the limelight for once.

The replay was an odd affair, looking back, as it was in the middle of the three-day week. The kick-off was bizarrely on a Wednesday afternoon due to the miners and electricity workers being on strike across the country as they battled with the government for better pay and conditions, so there was a need to conserve energy by not using the floodlights. There was also the added bonus of knowing that the winners would be facing Liverpool at home in the next round, but although that idea was tempting all our thoughts were on Leeds. We went up a few days beforehand and although the game was tight at first we knew that the longer we kept them out from scoring the crowd would get on their backs, except of course the several thousand Bristol City fans who had skipped work to travel up to Yorkshire. The Wills Tobacco company in Bedminster, the biggest employer in south Bristol, even shut down production for the duration of the game so fans could listen on the radio.

There was definitely a tougher approach from Leeds. I'm not saying they went easy on us at Ashton Gate but perhaps they now knew what we were about and they knew they would be in for a tough 90 minutes. We weathered storm after storm but it was like the Alamo, it was relentless as the Leeds forward line came at us in wave after wave. Every time we cleared the ball away or sorted out danger we shouted to each other and gave encouragement. To have gone in at half-time 0-0 was nothing short of a miracle considering the pressure we were under. We were aware that the Leeds fans were starting to get on their players' backs as their attacks broke down and we could also hear the section of City fans singing at the top of their voices.

The second half was more of the same and then with around 15 minutes to go Keith Fear picked up the ball in midfield and slotted a pass through to Donnie Gillies, who was running towards goal with Norman Hunter. Donnie wrapped his left foot around the ball and his shot crashed into the net, leaving keeper Harvey stranded. We just couldn't believe it as we ran towards him to celebrate and then we realised we still had the rest of the game to go. I remember asking referee Jack Taylor, 'How long to go?' He replied, 'Enough time,' and I then proceeded to ask him almost every minute as the clock ran down. When the whistle blew there was a mixture of relief and joy.

When I'm asked now about certain games I played in that stick in the memory, those two against Leeds are always up there.

I can honestly that say I enjoyed every minute of them, mainly I think as there was no pressure on us.

The result was a turning point for us as we suddenly believed that maybe we could do something in the coming seasons. The dressing room was chaos as champagne flowed and I remember our old chief scout Tony Collins, who was now at Leeds, being furious at his team's defeat. He was really angry, saying that we were lucky and the goal was a fluke. The more angry he got the more I laughed. Tony was a great guy and he knew football inside out but that day I think he was in shock. Then through the bedlam Liverpool boss Bill Shankly came in and had a laugh, particularly with the Scottish lads, who ribbed him mercilessly over his pre-match comments of what a great game Leeds United v Liverpool would be in the quarter-final. He left by telling us we had 'nae chance in the next round'.

When we eventually got back to Bristol we went straight out to celebrate. We didn't go to the Platform One nightclub which was our usual haunt in the centre of Bristol; instead we went to a pub in Long Ashton just outside the city as we knew the landlord so he kept it open for us. My defining memory of that night is that the pub had an outside toilet which Donnie Gillies went to use and I never saw him again. Apparently he had fallen in some bushes and spent the night there, probably dreaming of his match-winning goal.

The buzz was still around Bristol and across the UK regarding the giant-killing as Liverpool came to town. I was reeling from a problem with my ankle and although I was involved in the build-up and was relishing playing against Kevin Keegan, who I thought would suit me down to the ground, in the back of my mind there was a fear that I wouldn't make the game. I had missed our home game with Oxford United due to the injury and I knew it would go to the wire. On the morning of the match I had a fitness test with Alan Dicks and Les Bardsley looking on, but it was not right so I was not going to play. I was gutted and so were the lads, even though some of them said that I only used my right ankle for keeping me upright as I was all left foot. I enjoyed the banter but deep down I was really disappointed not to be running out with them.

I hung around for a bit but a couple of hours ahead of the game I left the ground and had a cup of tea with Mum and Dad, returning just before the start so I could see the lads before they went out. As I walked back to the ground among all the fans in my suit, they were all shouting that I was late and they were really disappointed that I wasn't playing. I am a terrible spectator and the 90 minutes were nothing short of gruelling as I headed and kicked every ball from the grandstand. We lost 1-0 to a John Toshack header, but we had done fantastically well against two top teams and I was very proud of the lads and the way they had handled themselves both in the build-up and on the pitch. It was at least some comfort that Liverpool went on to win the FA Cup that year by beating Newcastle 3-0 in the final.

After the excitement of the cup run it was back to reality in the league, where our form was patchy to say the least and we finished the season in a disappointing 16th place. The cup run had certainly saved Alan Dicks's job. I really feel that if we had not had that run he would have been sacked, and Alan would be the first person to tell you that himself.

When I look back, it was great to be pitting our wits against such top sides and also be recognised by the country's media as a decent team. It was brilliant to be in the spotlight but I wanted it to continue and I wanted to get to the top with the club I loved more than anything.

6

A Wanted Man

WITH THE season gone I spent two weeks of the summer on holiday with Wendy and Charlotte in Tunisia. It was a wonderful time as we relaxed by the pool and swam in the sea. It was important to recharge your batteries and I certainly did that. I also enjoyed the fact that I could just be Geoff the man and not Geoff the footballer, which was the case until I remember sitting alongside Wendy in the hotel lobby when I saw this guy with his family. I looked a bit closer and it then dawned on me that it was Bobby Campbell, who was a coach at Arsenal. Bobby was a wing-half back in the day for his hometown club Liverpool and then Portsmouth before injury finished his career, which is why he took up coaching.

He was also on holiday and suddenly he looked up and saw me, so immediately came over along with his wife and children and we talked football. During the holiday we met up a few times around the pool or at the beach and our two families got on really well. Bobby was chatting about how Bristol City had done that previous season and why we seemed to have struggled in the league. He also talked about the famous FA Cup games against Leeds United and Liverpool, as well as telling me about how things were going at Arsenal and that he had seen me play a few times and how impressed he was. I really just put it down to politeness on his part as I never for one moment thought he had been down to Ashton Gate to watch me.

After a great holiday we said our goodbyes to Bobby and his family and returned to Bristol ready for the pre-season. I had enjoyed the brief spell I had with Bobby but I certainly never thought how pivotal that meeting would be in the seasons to come. Pre-season was always tough as back then the main thing was running, and I mean a lot of running. We would be in at around 10am and finish about 2pm. I'm not going to say it was tough like working in a coal mine or any other full-time job but it was still challenging nonetheless.

Our favourite running place was Ashton Court, which was a large house in grounds on the edge of Bristol. The roads were up and down and we seemed to be on them all day, of course with the super-fit Gerry Sweeney in the lead. When we eventually got to Ashton Gate we would be sprinting on the cinder track that went around the pitch. It was relentless and I'm not ashamed to say that some afternoons I would arrive at my house in Backwell unable to get out of the bloody car, I was that knackered, but the team was built on fitness and I'm sure there was no fitter team in that division than us.

For the new season there was no talk of promotion, just a feeling that we had to do better than finishing 16th as we had done in 1973/74. We knew the season would be tough especially with Manchester United taking their place in the Second Division after being relegated, and mix them in with the likes of Norwich City, Aston Villa, Sunderland, West Brom and Southampton and it was always going to be tough to get near the top. The main excitement for the campaign was over what Paul Cheesley would do in his first full season for the Robins. Paul was a Bristol lad who had been poached away by Norwich as a youngster. He had done well at Norwich under manager Ron Saunders but after Saunders was replaced by John Bond, Paul found his opportunities reduced so Alan Dicks had moved in to sign him for £30,000 in December 1973. Paul had played a few games and you could see that he was just what we needed up front – he was confident and outspoken at times and I think deep down he wanted to prove that he was sold far too early by Norwich.

Alan had also let Bobby Gould go and much as I liked Bobby, he just didn't really fit in. We used to call him 'Snip' as when he would score in training he would shout out to Alan that he had been signed for a snip. It was pure Bobby, full of confidence. He and Alan had fallen out regarding an away game we had at Hull City, which we had lost 2-1. We stayed overnight in a hotel and all the players were having a few drinks before heading off to bed as it got later and later. There were a few players left and they decided that they were hungry so they went to the kitchen to cook something, but left it in a right state. Come morning, when the hotel manager arrived he was banging on Alan's door to tell him what had happened. On our return to Ashton Gate, Alan and his staff got us all in the changing rooms and asked us who did the damage. Nobody said a thing even though many of the lads had gone to bed early and clearly were not involved in the incident. He said that if anybody was not a part of what had happened they could leave at that moment, but again nobody moved or said anything. With that Alan said he was fining everybody £20 and then Bobby got up and said he wasn't involved and he would not be paying a fine.

I could see that Bobby did not want to get the blame for something he didn't do, but Alan saw it as a weak link in the dressing room spirit where players would have the backs of their team-mates, and that was something on which our promotion team was based. Days later, Bobby put in a transfer request and was sold to West Ham United.

The difference with Paul was that he was much more a team player on and off the field. After all, he was one of the founding members of F-Troop: Paul, Ray Cashley, Brian Drysdale, Gerry Gow, Donnie Gillies and Gerry Sweeney. F-Troop were the unofficial social committee and a group of lads who would always be the last ones standing when we went out for a drink. We had some fantastic times together and some things we did I really can't put in a book, so I'm sorry to disappoint. We were no angels when we went out but the strength of the team spirit was immense; not only were we team-mates but we were friends who knew each other's families and we would do anything for each other. If we were going out we all went out together and nobody was left behind.

The only other new members of the squad were midfielder Jimmy Mann, who Alan signed from Leeds United, and goalkeeper John Shaw, also from Leeds. It was great business from Alan as they were both on free transfers with John being competition in the future for Ray Cashley. They both fitted in really well and that showed the talent Alan and his team had for getting in just the right players who would enhance a dressing room rather than disrupt it.

With the optimism running through the side it was a real disappointment when we had a terrible start in the league campaign, drawing 0-0 with Nottingham Forest and then doing the same with Leyton Orient, then losing 2-0 to Oldham Athletic. It was particularly disappointing as we had looked so good in pre-season, but looking back on 1974/75 there are a still a few highs. I remember we played Liverpool in the League Cup, drawing 0-0 at home then losing 4-0 at Anfield. For me it was great to at last play against Kevin Keegan and he did suit me as even though he was a great player he never had a kick in either match. Although we lost up at Anfield as a side we played well and got a great reception from the fans after the game and in the press.

There was still paper talk about clubs coming in for me but I just put it to the back of my mind. It seemed that speculation was always going to be there but I just believed in Bristol City and knew I could achieve things with them. During this season there was also a great win at Eastville against neighbours Bristol Rovers in the league. We were 1-0 down at half-time with the wind against us, then the second half with the wind with us we scored four goals. Rovers had Alan Warboys and Bruce Bannister up front, or 'Smash and Grab' as they were called in the press due to their goalscoring exploits, but Gary Collier and I always had them in our back pockets, so they were never a problem.

I wanted to mention Rovers as the rivalry in the city is there today but it doesn't seem as passionate as it used to be. I remember when I was watching those games as a youngster from the terraces as well as playing against them in the youth team and even the reserves, the crowds were massive and it was the one match you just had to win so your supporters would have bragging rights for a couple of months. There are probably many reasons why the fixtures are not so big now, perhaps things like a lack of local lads playing for both clubs and the teams being so far apart in terms of league position so they never really meet in a competitive fixture. Back in my time they would also meet every season in the Gloucester Cup, which was played at the end of the season. It was a fixture that the players loved and at the time the supporters did too but fans fell out of love for it and it doesn't happen now, which is a shame.

I always loved playing Rovers and particularly at Eastville where there was a great atmosphere for derby games. I am sure that more fans came to the Eastville games than to those at Ashton Gate, probably because they were always in our shadow as a club, and I say that tongue in cheek! Off the field I never had any problem with Rovers fans. Don't get me wrong, they would give me a bit of stick, but it was never malicious, and that was the same with the players. Rovers defender Frankie Prince was a really good mate of mine and had a fierce reputation for taking no prisoners when he played. Although we were mates he would do his best to kick me up in the air whenever he got the chance in matches. The Rovers lads would also socialise with us, usually in the Platform One nightclub. It would certainly make fans take a second look when they saw us all together but that was how things were back then.

Although we finished a remarkable fifth in the league that year, looking back the season is littered with what ifs. We lost Paul Cheesley to injury and if I'm honest indifferent form as Alan chopped and changed things up front, the result being that Paul only played 13 games for us so he just couldn't get started. Donnie Gillies, who could play anywhere, finished our highest scorer with ten goals so you could see that we lacked firepower up front. Another huge miss through injury was the influential midfielder Gerry Gow, who I am sure only played around 20 games that season due to Achilles tendon and cartilage problems when usually he was an ever-present. There were back-to-back wins against the eventual champions Manchester United, who went up with Aston Villa. After our victories over United, their manager Tommy Docherty went to town on us, telling the press that we were the most negative side they had ever faced. After the game at Old Trafford, their captain Martin Buchan told me in the bar that Tommy was furious with being beaten by a bunch of 'country bumpkins' as he had called us in their dressing room. To Martin's credit, he also talked for ages about how good we were and he thought we had a real chance of promotion.

We were really in the mix with a few weeks to go but defeat against Norwich and a draw at home to Bristol Rovers around Easter left us just off the pack. Our season was finally over after a 1-0 defeat away at Leyton Orient where all hopes were dashed. That game sticks in my mind for many reasons, one of which is that at that point it was my biggest disappointment in league football. There was a floodlight failure at 0-0 and I led the team off under the instruction of Alan Dicks, who wanted us back in the dressing room to keep warm as there would be a 20-minute delay. At the time the Orient fans thought that I was trying to get the game abandoned by taking the team off so I got a ton of abuse from the crowd. In the end both teams had to leave the field on the say-so of the referee, which settled the crowd down a bit. They couldn't fully fix the lights so the game restarted with them on at half power. I also remember having a massive tussle with Derek Possee, who was a top-class striker and always gave me problems when we played each other. Derek was quick and would get stuck in to you from the off. He wasn't a big man but he really put himself about, and he got the goal after a mistake from me.

When the game ended I was distraught and did not want to speak to anyone. I blamed myself for the error and blamed myself for Bristol City not going up, which plainly wasn't the case, but that's how I am. It stayed with me for days and I can honestly say that it was the worst coach journey home I have ever had in my football career. There was silence and I just did not want to speak or engage with anybody around me. All I wanted was my car and my front door and for me to get behind it as quickly as I could. It took ages for the disappointment to leave me.

Looking back at the league campaign, if things had gone in our favour we could have gone up. We were seven points behind second place, which looking at it now wasn't bad. The squad were together in every way and even though we didn't want to get ahead of ourselves, the fans started to think that maybe we were on the brink of something.

Our season ended with a tour of Norway and I was happy to at last be able to join the lads overseas. Alan liked taking us to Norway, plainly not for his tan but the teams there at that time were into their season so the matches were competitive, although you wouldn't have thought so with the standard of opposition. We were due to play four games across the country and the worst part was that the planes kept getting smaller the further we travelled. A lot of the lads were bad flyers, and in particular Gerry Gow hated it. He was always last on the plane and that always meant the last man on board had to shut the door so we always checked after Gerry had done it.

We criss-crossed Norway, sometimes landing side-on at the top of a mountain to reach the various opponents we had lined up. We beat Molde 2-0, Bodø-Glimt 1-0, and FK Mjølner 5-2. But the real performance was our 10-0 win against Mo. I scored two goals, which was a rarity, and although the opposition were not great we absolutely played them off the pitch which was so great for our confidence, let alone mine.

The trips abroad were brilliant for team bonding. We would all be together, and those tours were an excellent way at creating an atmosphere of unity. We would to a certain extent get away from football and get to know each other as mates, talking about our ambitions, our families and everyday life. It was also really important for the new lads or those who had come up from the youth team to be themselves and form strong friendships with other players. It was also a chance to clear the air with people and that certainly happened a few times. Many a time there would be a difference of opinion but we had an environment where things would not be allowed to fester – they would be nipped in the bud straight away as you knew you could say your piece and that was it.

F-Troop were at the thick of things during the tour although never in the hotel as beer was £1 a pint, which was a fortune back then. They did, however, manage to find a bar in town where it was 35p so normal service was resumed. I would love to go into depth regarding some of the antics that went on but I'm sure you will agree that what happens on tour stays on tour. We got into all sorts of scrapes but we were always conscious that we were representing Bristol City Football Club, which would be more emphasised when we would be asked to put the blazers and ties on and do the rounds with the local dignitaries as I would be asked to give a speech and talk for the players. I never minded as I was so proud to be the captain. When the tour ended we were back to family holidays and I of course would fit in some time working on the farm.

We hit the start of 1975/76 running. There was no pre-season tour and instead we just played a few friendlies, notably against Cardiff City and Hereford United. We won them both with ease and the excitement was building as Paul Cheesley was partnered with Tom Ritchie up front and they had hit it off right from the word go. Paul in particular was on fire in front of goal. The confidence seemed to sweep through the side and in the autumn we found ourselves in the mix at the top of the table along with the favourites West Brom, Sunderland and Southampton. In the November we featured on *Match of the Day* as we put York City to the sword 4-1 with a goal from me and Tom scoring a hat-trick. It was great to be in the national limelight again and I would love to say we were all sat at home watching ourselves that Saturday night, but in reality we were probably celebrating together along with our wives at Platform One.

As we turned into 1976 the rumours and stories in the press regarding offers from other clubs became non-stop, not only for me but for all the lads. There were bids in for Gerry Gow from Celtic and Ipswich Town. Ipswich were managed by Bobby Robson, who was a big admirer of Gerry and had tried to get him on numerous occasions. As far as Gerry was concerned, he said he had no wish to leave the club, especially as the season was going really well for us. There were also newspaper stories of interest for our young winger Clive Whitehead from Coventry City and Norwich. Clive had only just broken into the first team from the youth side and you could see he had bags of potential. Luton Town, Everton and Coventry were reported to be interested in our young centre-back Gary Collier, who was a class act. We were all open regarding these stories and we would chat before training about what was in the paper that day, but the general feedback was that nobody really wanted to go anywhere.

Among all of this was a reported massive bid from Arsenal for myself and Tom Ritchie. This story is one that always gets told when talking about Geoff Merrick the footballer and I'm glad I have the opportunity, like with some of the other events later in my career, to give an honest account of it. The Arsenal speculation had been brewing in the paper for some time. Me and Tom just laughed it off and got some stick from the lads about it. I can't speak for Tom but this was how it played out for me. Arsenal were managed by Bertie Mee and had won the Double in 1971. Bertie had started to rebuild his team as a lot of the Double-winning side were getting older and making way for new players. Arsenal had finished a disappointing 16th in the First Division the previous season so they were very much in a state of transition. I had met Bobby Campbell, their first team coach, on holiday and I could now see that maybe Bobby wasn't just being polite when he said he had been following me at City. The press speculation grew and grew and it got to the point where I went to see Alan Dicks regarding whether there was anything in it as the club didn't say anything about it either privately or publicly. Alan said yes, Arsenal had been in touch and had offered £240,000, which had been rejected but City were sure there would be a further offer. I was gutted.

Alan explained that finances were not great at that moment and the club had Gary Collier and Dave Rodgers at the back who could easily replace me. It was like a punch in the stomach; hearing that I could be replaced was the last thing I wanted. I loved the club and the idea of leaving, particularly at that time in the season, when we were so close to promotion, was hard to take.

I spoke at length to Wendy and I told her I had no desire to go to London. I know if I had wanted the move she would have supported me in an instant. I know it seems funny but when I thought about it I would wonder what I would do in London and think that I would miss the farm work. To make matters worse, my good friend Peter Godsiff, the *Bristol Evening Post* writer, had written two pieces for the paper. One was an interview with chairman Robert Hobbs which ran under the headline 'ARSENAL BID. IT'S UP TO THE FANS'. In it, Hobbs said, 'The supporters will really decide whether Geoff Merrick and Tom Ritchie will be sold to Arsenal as we need more people through the gates. We are losing £2,000 a week and we could save the club £500 a week if we clear our £200,000 overdraft. We do really have to sell, particularly when you look at our last home game against Blackburn Rovers which brought in just 12,000 fans. Arsenal have been pursuing both players from the start of the season but a firm offer is on the table. It's up to the players now as I know Alan Dicks does not want them to leave as it could scupper our promotion chances.' Then a few days later the headline was 'MERRICK WILL GO'. The article said that I was on my way to Arsenal and the deal for me and Tom could go ahead in the coming days.

Apparently the club were happy to let me go as there was defensive cover in Collier and Rodgers, and also Brian McNeill was just coming through from the youth team and could cover midfield. As for replacing Tom up front, the article continued with the news that the club were looking to bring in former Swindon Town player Don Rodgers, who was now at QPR, or Derby's Alan Hinton as potential new signings.

I was far from happy and I demanded a meeting with Robert Hobbs, who I got on really well with. I went in to see him and Alan and I just told them I had no interest in Arsenal and it could be really damaging to the promotion campaign which was coming into a crucial period. Alan agreed that he did not want me or Tom to go. With that, Robert decided he would look at my contract and on the spot told me that he would link my wages with the *Financial Times* Index, so if it went up then so would my wages. To be honest, I had no idea what he was talking about but I think I was about £20 better off a week. I came out of the meeting with something but to this day I'm not sure what.

This period in my career is always mentioned and its seems to some people that I wasn't allowed to go to Arsenal, as though the club held me back. The truth is that I never wanted to go. If I had then I could have made things difficult for Bristol City, but it never entered my mind. I was happy and that was all that mattered. I was the captain of the greatest football team in the world in my eyes so why would I go anywhere else? I'm sure there was more money on offer at Arsenal but it made no difference to me. I needed to be happy and when you compare it to today's football it seems crazy that I wouldn't go from the Second Division to the First Division and join a club like Arsenal, but that's how I felt.

I liken it to the stick Matt Le Tissier got for not leaving Southampton for a big club; people said he had no ambition but again he was happy. I had the same sort of comments from Peter Osgood, who I had met many times through Chris Garland at Chelsea. I remember a couple of days after the news had broken that I was staying we drew 1-1 with promotion rivals Southampton at home. Osgood was now at Southampton and I got stuck in to him, which he didn't like, so he decided to try and wind me up by saying, 'You're a bottler, Merrick, you were too afraid to mix it with the big boys in the top division.' I took it all in my stride and I didn't care what other fans or players thought about my decision. What I wanted more than ever was to prove everybody wrong and show that my loyalty to Bristol City was going to pay off with promotion to the big time.

7

A Dream Come True

AS SPECULATION on my future died down, we were left within touching distance of the First Division. We were becoming difficult to beat and at times were winning ugly. As we entered March we went on a run of seven games without defeat, which included two pivotal fixtures in the promotion season of 1975/76.

The first was away at front-runners West Bromwich Albion. Albion were always a good side and always seemed to be either gaining promotion to the top flight or getting relegated from it. Their manager was Johnny Giles, the ex-Leeds United midfielder, and the team were very much in his mould; they were hard and tough but could play as well. The fixture was rearranged as the original game some weeks earlier was called off by the FA as we had around nine lads out with flu, so we couldn't field a full team. I was one and I could have played if I'm honest but the club said, 'No, you're ill,' so that was that.

The match was what you would have expected from two teams who were both fighting for promotion. We were on top in the first half and got the breakthrough just on half-time with a brilliant goal from Gerry Sweeney. That forced West Brom to come at us in the second half but we weathered the storm and at one point Paul Cheesley broke through with only the keeper to beat, but he just placed the ball wide of the post. It was unusual as Paul was on fire in the league up to that game and I remember watching him go through from back in our half and thinking 'that's it, 2-0'. But we hung on to win and it really sent out a message to the other clubs in the division that we were still in the mix fighting.

The second game was Sunderland away. They were top of the league if I remember rightly and we went up a few days before as we knew how big the match was going to be for us. We were boosted by Paul choosing to play for us instead of for the England under-23 side, who were facing Hungary at Old Trafford the same night. It was a tremendous thing for Paul to do and it showed how together we were as a unit.

Sunderland's Roker Park was a massive ground and it was full that night with over 40,000 fans. Our aim was to keep it tight and try to silence the crowd, which we did in the first half. It was a scary type of silence that came over the ground and when we went 1-0 up just after half-time through that man Gerry Sweeney, you could have heard a pin drop around the ground. I think the Sunderland fans couldn't believe that they were actually losing the game. The team put pressure on us with wave after wave of attacks and then with about 15 minutes to go they got a goal and the place erupted. The 'Roker roar', as it was known, was incredible and it was the loudest crowd I have ever played in front of in my life.

The noise and pressure on us over the last couple of minutes was overwhelming, and to be honest I didn't want the ball as I did not want to make a mistake and cost us the game, so when the ref blew for full time I was glad it was over but we were disappointed as the draw really did feel like a defeat, but after a few hours we realised what an achievement it was to take a point off them in their own back yard.

After the game we stayed in the hotel for a few days before travelling up to Carlisle United where we won 1-0 through a Gerry Gow penalty. We knew that we were so close to achieving all our dreams. We never really talked about promotion as we just thought on to the next game, then once that was done we looked to the next one, but I remember the following week sitting at home with Wendy. I was sat in a red rocking chair that she had bought me, sipping on a Guinness and watching the news when the sports results came up and I think Sunderland had lost away. It was then that it hit me and I turned to Wendy and said, 'I really think we are going to get promoted.' It was a really odd feeling that hit me. I don't know if it was a sudden rush of adrenaline or pressure but suddenly I thought, 'This is real, we could be in the First Division.' It was a feeling I never told anybody about and I just kept it to myself.

As the run-in started we had a bit of a bumpy few games, losing to Blackpool then drawing against Chelsea and Bristol

Rovers, but other results had gone our way and we needed two points from our last two games to go up. The next match was Portsmouth at home, where a win would send us up in to the First Division so the excitement among the players, staff and fans started days before.

Alan Dicks was a superstitious man so we tried to keep everything the same as normal. He even had a lucky suit, which he wore. The local papers were building the match up with what it might be like having a Bristol team in the top flight and there were different interviews with many ex-City players and various local celebrities, who all wished us well.

Tuesday, 20 April 1976 was a beautiful warm day and I remember thinking that it could be the day when everything comes together as we all met at the Ashton Court Country Club on the outskirts of the city. The idea was to have a light training session then some lunch and stay among the grounds until we had to get on the coach and drive the couple of miles to Ashton Gate. We were totally relaxed, and I was somebody who did suffer from nerves before games, but on this day I had none and even now I still don't know why. Everybody knew what this match meant to the red half of the city. We could create history.

Being so serenely calm was odd for me. I have tried to analyse how I felt many times and I have seen reports of Formula One racing drivers who get so 'in the zone' that they forget all around them and are almost on autopilot in terms of doing their job. That's how I felt and I still think about it today. To pass the time,

I played snooker with Brian Drysdale and we had a real laugh mainly at each other's attempts to take good shots. There were guest at the hotel and I was talking to them, explaining what the prize was for the evening's game, and they wished us well which created a fabulous atmosphere before we left.

Going to the ground in a sea of red and white scarves, flags and banners was incredible. When the fans saw us they were singing and shouting up at us as we waved from the coach. If we didn't know how much this meant to them beforehand, we certainly knew on our way to the stadium. There was a carnival atmosphere inside and around Ashton Gate. On the way to the dressing room you could see all the various members of staff who worked there. They were cheering us and you really felt the responsibility. Again, I felt no nerves; I was supremely focused. I just wanted to lead the team out and get going.

Our opponents, Portsmouth, were already relegated so it was really difficult to work out how they would set up. They had lots of youngsters but halso a few old heads in the side who were never going to lie down and let us walk all over them. All the pressure was on us and although I was not nervous, some of the lads clearly were. You could see on their faces that this was the big one.

We walked out at Ashton Gate to a massive wall of noise on a lovely warm evening and we were certainly raring to go. We started well and incredibly after about five minutes Clive Whitehead found space on the edge of Portsmouth's box and he fired the ball straight into the net. The place erupted and it was chaos as we all ran towards Clive, who was under a pile of City shirts. When things settled down we knew we had to concentrate on the rest of the game. Looking back now, I know it sounds crazy but I wonder if we scored too soon as from that point we just played terribly. The nerves were clearly going through the whole side. I remember slicing a ball, admittedly with my right foot, across our goal and keeper Ray Cashley had to scramble back to stop it going in the net. We didn't play well and speaking to the lads even today they all say that it really was a terrible performance from us. Having said that we kept Portsmouth out and to their credit they gave it a real go.

It was the longest 90 minutes I have ever played in – it seemed to go on for eternity. As the clocked ticked on I could sense the crowd getting nearer and nearer to the pitch. I think they were about three rows deep pitchside. I said to the referee Mr Homewood, 'You have got to blow the whistle soon mate because if Portsmouth score we are not going to get out of this ground alive.' After my comments, Portsmouth had a goal kick and as the ball went up into the night sky the final whistle blew and Ashton Gate went wild.

The euphoria I felt in that moment is something I can't really do justice to this book, and just thinking about that moment now fills me with butterflies in my stomach and tears in my eyes. The surge of excitement and adrenaline that rushed through me, I have never experienced anything like it since. This was the ultimate dream for me since I was seven years of age and we had done it.

People around me were sobbing – men, women, youngsters, older fans. I thought about all the players who had played for the club over the years. I thought about my mum and dad. I eventually ran to my mate Brian Drysdale and we just embraced with a combination of exhaustion and relief. The crowd swarmed on to the pitch, grabbing us and kissing us, and I will never forget their faces – they were overjoyed and caught up in the moment as we all were.

The rest of the players were dotted all over the pitch under all the fans' celebrations but we eventually broke free and ran for the tunnel. When I got to the tunnel I was met by striker Keith Fear, who was not in the side. We grabbed each other and I immediately thought of Keith and the other players who had helped us in the season yet didn't play that night. Keith is a wonderful man and I know how disappointed he was not to be picked but like all of the lads he supported us from the bench, so it was their night as well as the 11 on the pitch.

When I eventually got to the dressing room it was chaos, with about 50 people in there all singing and drinking champagne. The local TV cameras were crammed in there trying to get a few words with players but we were just singing and letting our hair down. If I'm honest, I was in a state of shock. We threw Alan Dicks into the bath and all got called up to the Williams Stand to wave to the fans. It was one of my proudest moments in life, looking down on a sea of red and white that covered the pitch. Alan made a speech and so did I but when I look at that clip now

I just look stunned by the whole thing. I wasn't flying high or anything, I just think the realisation had not yet hit me. I think maybe that was the enormity of the situation kicking in. Looking down at the fans, I could see what it meant to them. We were a family and as captain I was one of the heads of it.

As a club, we were always on the outside looking in at top-flight football. Yes, we had a good FA Cup run, but we were always considered a footballing backwater and now we were at the top table and were going to mix it with the likes of Liverpool and both Manchester clubs as well as Everton and Arsenal. It was an incredible sense of achievement.

We had used 17 players that season and 11 had come through the youth ranks at the club, which was phenomenal. I think people forget that when talking about that side. Myself, Ray Cashley, Gerry Gow, Trevor Tainton and Tom Ritchie had played every game of the season, which again was a fantastic record. Many of the lads had also turned down interest from other clubs along the journey as they dreamed about this night and achieving things with Bristol City. It was a wonderful feeling to be vindicated in our decision not to leave.

After getting showered and changed, all the lads met up with our wives and made our way to the supporters' bar. It was rammed with people, many of whom worked at the club or had supported Bristol City for years; many were in tears and it was so humbling for them to be thanking us for, in their words, the best night of their lives. Wendy and I stayed for a few drinks but then went to my mother's to pick up our daughter Charlie and we drove home to Backwell. When I got home I made a very emotional phone call to my brother Vernon, who was in Berlin and desperate for news on how City had done. He wished me well and told me how proud of me he was, which meant so much to me. So as all the lads went and painted the city red, I sat at home with Wendy reflecting on what we had achieved.

When I woke up the next day there was a massive feeling of almost anti-climax. I know that sounds strange but everything I had ever wanted to achieve in football I had now done, and I was genuinely thinking, 'What now?' It was, looking back, as though I was just feeling flat now we had got to the promised land.

My whole attitude had changed. When I was younger all I had to do was look after myself and make sure Alan Dicks was impressed enough to pick me, and when I was captain I worried about the whole team, but now this seemed so much bigger. I thought about the people on the board, the people who worked at the club and how if we didn't stay in the top flight they could lose their jobs. I felt a massive wave of pressure and responsibility on me as to making sure the club could now stay in the First Division, plus there was a real sense of anxiety over what lay ahead in the coming seasons, so much so that before the season started I went and spoke to the club doctor Mr Fowler about how I was feeling. He said that it was a natural thing to be worried and that I'd had a massive release of adrenaline and pressure from the previous season, but he felt that over the years it would be something I would learn to cope with. I'm not sure he was right but it certainly helped being able to talk with him about how I felt.

Back then I never told the lads as they would probably have taken the piss, not out of any malice but talking about those thoughts was just something you did not do then, and if I'm honest it would have been thought of as a sign of weakness, especially from the team captain. I'm sure that would not be the case in today's football but that's how things were back then.

As the club still celebrated our achievement I would like to say that things calmed down before our last match of the season against Notts County, but they didn't. South Bristol was still in party mood and the Bristol press were filled with page upon page about our promotion and the First Division stars who would be coming to Ashton Gate the following season. As the players met for the Notts County game, the dressing room was buzzing with stories of what we all got up to in terms of celebrating. We were all taking the mick and really enjoying going out to play our last game. I think we still had a chance of pipping Sunderland to the title but as far as the fans were concerned we had done it and they just wanted us to put on a show. This match, even today, gets to me as we lost 2-1. I know the lads had been out and celebrated really hard and maybe that was the reason for our defeat, but we certainly were not unprofessional in our approach. When the game was over the dressing room was like a morgue and the club arranged for us to do a lap of honour, which some of the lads really didn't want to do as it's difficult doing that when you have just been beaten at home, irrespective of promotion. But I led them out anyway and it was a hollow feeling. It felt as though we had spoiled the fans' party. Sunderland went up as champions with 56 points. We finished second with 53, along with West Bromwich Albion who also had 53. Bolton Wanderers just missed out on 52 points.

The council arranged a open-top bus parade for us around the streets of south Bristol, culminating in a reception with the lord mayor and other dignitaries at the Council House. It was a fantastic occasion as we drove through the streets of Bedminster, Ashton, Whitchurch and Knowle. I was immensely proud as these were my people and we were visiting the places I had grown up in, so to have crowds of people cheering and waving with flags and scarves, some from the tops of trees and lampposts, was a wonderful sight. When I look at the film of it today I am mesmerised by my sheepskin coat that I had on. At the time I thought I really looked the business but anybody who watches the clips today always says to me, 'Where the bloody hell did you get that coat, Geoff?' Even Neil, who has helped me write this book, said that if Bristol City had a museum that coat should be in it. If it happens, I will have to get it from the dog as he sleeps in it now.

I made a speech at the Council House balcony addressing the fans, and thankfully I had taken my coat off at that point. I said something along the lines of, 'After travelling around the city you people deserve as much credit as we do. You have been absolutely tremendous.' After that we were all introduced to various people, who I never really felt relaxed around. The only way I can put it is that they were all posh. Harry Dolman's wife Marina was there and she was introducing me to various people around the room. I love Marina dearly and she is a wonderful friend to me even today. She has always been supportive towards me, right from when I signed for the club as a kid, and she made it easier for me around those sort of people.

Our season was now over but I had one more match to see – the FA Cup Final between Southampton and Manchester United. I had got two tickets through the club and I decided to go up to Wembley and watch the game with my dad. It was a great day, especially for Second Division Southampton as they beat top-flight United with a goal from Bobby Stokes. I was pleased for Bobby as our paths had crossed in youth team football, particularly in the England trials. It was a special day for him and it was a tragedy that he died years later of pneumonia at the age of 44.

At the end of the game I was coming out of Wembley with dad when I bumped into Bobby Campbell. He congratulated me on promotion and we laughed and chatted as I introduced him to Dad. Bobby said to me that I should have gone to Arsenal. I told him I had no desire to go and he said, 'All you had to do was call us and we would have signed you straight away.' I was flattered but as I said to him, it just wasn't my style to go phoning a club when I was already at another. We shook hands and went our separate ways. I thought about what he said and knew I had made the right choice.

There was no let-up for the captain of Bristol City in the hot summer of 1976. Myself and Wendy were invited to all sorts of events as I was now captain of a First Division club. I got given a sponsored car – a black Volkswagen Scirocco – by local travel agents Renwick's, who even sorted a cruise to the Mediterranean for me and the family that summer. Restaurants fell over backwards for you and people came out of the woodwork to offer you things or get to know you. I suppose it was part of being in the national limelight but it never really sat well with me. Don't get me wrong, it was great, but I was at my happiest with the cows on the farm.

When we returned for pre-season training it was plain to see that things were about to change within the club. There was talk of Alan Dicks getting a £5,000 bonus for promotion and we were getting £1,000, but I certainly never saw any of that. To my recollection we got a £50 a week bonus for getting to the First Division but it was stipulated that if we got relegated then the £50 would be withdrawn. Money was never really bandied about at Bristol City. We certainly never talked money and I honestly believe that the board never dreamed that the club would get to the top flight and therefore be in the big league in terms of wages.

I just felt that things were starting to unsettle us. In the dressing room, which had always been a tight-knit and open place among us players where money was never mentioned, there were now little conversations and whispers over what people were earning and questions about whether certain players had gone to the board on their own and negotiated a better deal for themselves. It was heartbreaking as on the way up to the big time we had never mentioned money. We knew we were all on different wages but it never bothered us. Among all this, you have to bear in mind that we had not even played in the First Division yet. There was a lot of tension and if you made a mistake in training there would be comments about not being worth your present salary. It wasn't just banter – there was a underlying feeling that all was not well.

I was one of the club's top earners at the time and I was on around £140 per week, which wasn't a fortune. There is no point comparing that to today's footballers as our pay would be a million miles away, but the average wage in 1976 was about £70 a week, so I was doing okay compared to the man in the street. Things blew up a few times between me and Gerry Gow as Gerry had heard, and I'm not sure from who, that I was on more money than he was. Gerry was fiery and I would give him as good back as he would give to me. It was crazy that we could have been arguing over, say, £20 when the real point was that we were going to be playing Arsenal at Highbury in our first game in the First Division.

I don't believe the club helped the situation and I think they caused a lot of it as they appeared to be trying to convince the public whenever they could through the TV and press that they had no money either and what they did have would now have to go on players' wages, which just wasn't true. So a lot of the players thought to themselves, 'I have not had any more money, I wonder who has?' and I think that's why the tension started in the dressing room. It infuriated me that the board would always mention that they were still losing money and it seemed that they were already preparing to be relegated and for life again in the Second Division, which was not what I as a captain wanted to hear. We were all paid well but it seemed they put this spin out that it was the players who were taking all the money out of the club.

If you look at it from the club's point of view, there was no TV money like today or merchandise to speak of. The income was from sponsors, of which they were many fighting over themselves to be part of Bristol City's First Division journey, and also gate receipts. Robert Hobbs once stated, when there was interest from Arsenal in me, that the club needed more fans to come through the turnstiles and they were losing money with gates of around 12,000. Now the club would be getting more sponsorship and double the gates, they were still pleading poverty to the fans and the media. It was a really difficult period leading up to our debut in the big time.

We patched things up as a team, particularly me and Gerry, as we were all open and honest with each other, but deep down I don't think that dressing room was ever really the same again and it wasn't the greatest of starts for our debut in the First Division.

8

Down to the Wire

A WARM Saturday afternoon in August 1976 will always hold a very special memory for me. The venue was Arsenal's ground, Highbury, and I had the privilege of being able to lead out my beloved Bristol City for their first match in the First Division. I have played in many of City's great games through the years but there was no feeling like it as a Bristol lad. I remember our lovely white away kit with the black shorts and socks, which was especially loved by Brian Drysdale as he said the socks made his legs look longer. We all felt a million dollars in it. The pitch was immaculate and the whole of the ground was an amazing cauldron of red and white.

Yes, the pre-season hadn't gone well with certain issues regarding money within the squad, but all of that was put behind us as we embarked on a new adventure. The trip along the M4 was incredible with car after car and coach after coach of City fans heading towards north London. I remember sitting in my usual seat at the front of the bus alongside physio Les Bardsley. In the adjoining seat was director Stephen Kew and as we came over the hill with the stadium in full view, he said, 'Wow, I have never seen so many City fans.' Although there were thousands I did have to tell him that Arsenal also played in red and white; that just showed how much your average director knew about football.

In the pre-season Arsenal had installed their former player Terry Neill as manager and broken the British transfer record by paying £333,000 for former Newcastle United and England centre-forward Malcolm Macdonald. 'Supermac', as he was known, had stated in the press that he was going to get off to a great start by bagging a few goals against newcomers Bristol City. As a team we just laughed it off but I for one knew that I would be up against it. Macdonald was an immensely powerful striker who was astonishingly quick and was incredible in the air. Despite this, we went into the game full of confidence, which was a result of promotion the previous season and Alan Dicks had kept the same side during the summer. I don't think we expected to win but we just wanted to make a good account of ourselves and we thought that if seven or eight of us had a good game we might be okay.

I have watched the game back on TV since. It was covered by ITV on their Sunday football show *The Big Match* with Brian Moore on commentary. When I watch it now you can't help but see that they really did not give us a chance and Moore's commentary is at the start quite condescending to the poor country side from Bristol. But as the game went on and we essentially played Arsenal off the park the commentary became more and more pro City. Every single player had a great game and Arsenal could not cope. Paul Cheesley was unplayable and although he got the goal in our 1-0 win he could easily have got three or four. It's a game that I enjoyed immensely. I remember I sat behind defender Gary Collier as we knew Macdonald was lethal running on to a through pass so that way I would be able to go with him and cut it out. It worked a treat as our midfield won everything so they stopped the supply.

I'm not sure if Arsenal took us for granted, but it's certainly been debated over the years that they did. It's a view that doesn't sit right with me as I feel it almost taints the great performance we gave. When the whistle blew for the end I was overjoyed. I remember grabbing hold of Gerry Gow and he said, 'I'm sorry about everything with the money.' I said 'me too' then we both looked at each other and in unison said, 'We have just beaten bloody Arsenal away.' We were deliriously happy but it was different to maybe a cup win. Of course we were the talk of the Sunday papers the following morning and the Bristol City fans were ecstatic but that was the division we were in now; it was just two points and nothing more. We were already concentrating on our next fixture and not revelling in the win like we may have if it had been an FA Cup tie. We were the same as Arsenal – both teams in the First Division. We weren't lucky and it wasn't a giant-killing, we were just better than they were and that was a great feeling, especially as Supermac had been in my back pocket all game.

Our home debut in the top flight was a midweek game against Stoke City at Ashton Gate. Stoke were a good side and included Peter Shilton in goal along with Jimmy Greenhoff, Alan Hudson and Garth Crooks. A crowd of 26,000 were there, which I'm sure must have pleased the directors that the red half of Bristol had come out to support First Division football. It ended 1-1 with Stoke scoring late on to deny us a win but the match will always be remembered for the injury to Paul Cheesley. During the first half, Paul went up for a challenge with Shilton. Paul landed awkwardly and although he went off injured, us players and the fans never realised the extent of the damage. The injury was to his knee ligaments and the surrounding cartilage, which basically finished Paul's career, and although he tried to come back a few months later against Birmingham City he never played again after that.

I think losing Paul that August evening was a major factor in the downfall of Bristol City. As a player there was nobody to touch him – he was getting better and better and he would have easily got us 20 goals plus a season. Every team needs a forward like that, let alone one that has just got promoted to the First Division. The whole saga with Paul put a cloud over the lads and we all found it very difficult to get rid of.

In our first eight games we had won two lost three and drawn three. It wasn't bad but I know it could have been so much better with Paul in terms of putting away chances. That's said with no disrespect to Tom Ritchie and Donnie Gillies, who played up front, but Donnie wasn't an out-and-out goalscorer and Tom worked so well with Paul. They had scored 34 goals between them the previous season.

In October we faced Leicester City, who now had Chris Garland up front after a move away from Chelsea. I always kept in touch with Chris. We would speak on a Saturday night after games and we would always ask about how each other was playing. It was great to be up against him but I didn't really want to get stuck into him as he was a mate. That's probably not very professional but it was true. Chris was always difficult to play against. He was so strong and skilful and you could see he had got better as a player while with Chelsea. The match sticks in my mind, not only for Chris, but we lost 1-0 through a Frank Worthington goal and I injured my ankle and had to go off. This wasn't as a result of Chris tackling me and whacking me like he used to do when I played against him all those years previously when we were kids.

The injury kept me out for a few games, and when I did return it was not to be with the number six on my back. There was talk in the papers regarding Norman Hunter coming to the club as he wasn't happy at Leeds United, and Alan's assistant Tony Collins, who had returned to the club, was friends with him due to their time together at Leeds. Norman was a vastly experienced defender who had played for England and won many trophies in the game. It seemed he was going to sign for Southampton but a deal was done and he joined City instead. Norman was a great guy and moved his family down to Bristol from Yorkshire, which was a great sign that he would be fitting in with us. He certainly did that. He had a wealth of knowledge and he was a great help to all of us in the side.

The problem was Norman's arrival meant I would be moving to left-back, which I didn't want to do. Alan Dicks never spoke to me about the move in position; in fact Tony only said anything after I bumped into him at the training ground. Tony said I would be moving as Norman did not want to play anywhere other than in the centre of a back four. I told him I didn't want to move, especially as it would be at the expense of my mate Brian Drysdale, who would be out of the side. Tony was adamant and even told me that it could be a great chance for me as England were struggling for a left-back at the time and I could make that position my own. I knew that was bullshit. I took the number three shirt and just got on with it, although everybody at the club knew I was unhappy.

Deep down, I was hurt that Alan could just move me without an explanation and also it wasn't as if I wasn't doing my job in the number six shirt. If my form had been bad then maybe I could understand the decision. In hindsight, when I look back at my career, that was the moment I should have left the club. I don't mean throwing my toys out of the pram but my problem was I was far too loyal. I should have thought about what was best for Wendy and the kids and also for my career. There was still interest in me from other clubs such as Queens Park Rangers and Wolverhampton Wanderers but I was loyal to Bristol City.

I always felt that playing full-back was detrimental to my career. I felt I was always suited to playing at the back and in the centre of defence off the centre-half. I had all these emotions spinning round and I was gutted for Brian, who I felt had not even been given a chance to show what he could do in the First Division. He went out on loan to Reading before leaving the club and signing for Oxford United. I was also gutted that Alan and his backroom team thought I wasn't as good as Norman Hunter to play in the centre. I know he was more experienced but I was younger and knew the players like the back of my hand. So looking back it was a case of me doing anything Bristol City wanted if I thought it would help the club instead of putting myself first.

As the year came to an end we found ourselves struggling for consistency and this led to a worrying slide down the table. As well as Norman joining us, the club also signed Scottish midfielder Peter Cormack from Liverpool. Peter was very experienced and had also played for Hibernian and Nottingham Forest. Another addition was Chris Garland. Chris had left Leicester City under a cloud due to a training-ground bust-up with one of his team-mates. It made me laugh when he told me that before he signed, Alan had said to him that there was no more money at the club as it had all gone to Norman and Peter, which was plainly untrue but it was just a way of letting Chris and the players know that the club were still pleading poverty. Chris was an inspiration for us. He was a better player than in his first spell with the club and he was City through and through. He understood the club and it meant an awful lot to him.

As we went into the new year we all knew that we would be in for a fight for survival. I was still performing at left-back and I was pleased that I had not missed a game since the move. Outside of football I was overjoyed that Wendy was expecting twins very soon and I knew the birth would make our family complete. As we moved towards the business end of the season it seemed that relegation would be between five clubs and with three going down we knew it was backs to the wall stuff. Our main rivals were Tottenham Hotspur – who looked doomed already – Stoke City, Sunderland and Coventry City. We really had struggled and the confidence we had once had seemed to desert us as we lost by the odd goal here and there. That's what was so frustrating – the fact that we had played all the top clubs and nobody had really battered us and we had always given everyone a game. I remember the confidence of the promotion side, when we knew that if we were 1-0 down we would pull it back to 1-1 no matter what was on the clock and if we were 1-0 up we thought we would make it 2-0 in no time. So what we needed was a break or a change in our luck, particularly as our last five games were Manchester United, Leeds, Middlesbrough, Liverpool and finally Coventry.

That spark we needed was Chris Garland, who basically saved us in the run-in. He scored in our 1-1 draw at home with Manchester United, a game that was played in front of 30,000 fans at Ashton Gate, then produced the winner at home to Leeds in a 1-0 victory. These results gave us a real chance of avoiding the drop and were revelled in by the local and national press as they had not given us a hope looking at our run-in. To be honest, I didn't blame them. But we were certainly not home and dry and going into the next game away at Middlesbrough I was struggling with pain in my ankle. Usually if I had a niggle with an injury I just played through the pain as I did not want to let the side down but this was persistent and although I played some part in our dour 0-0 draw, I had to come off due to the injury.

For the team it was another point nearer survival, but things were starting to get on top of me. Wendy had given birth to Elliott and Luke prematurely, and Luke was fighting for his life as he had a problem with his kidneys. Wendy wasn't in great shape herself and due to the complications of the birth she found herself in Southmead Hospital with the boys for eight weeks. It really was a nightmare for all of us. My ankle problems, although insignificant compared to what was happening to the boys, just compounded the problem, so my head was all over the place.

Despite all of this, when it came to playing, I had to be true to myself and think about the team and I knew that I was not going to be fit to play against Liverpool. From a selfish point of view, I suppose I could have played but it was such an important game that I knew I couldn't let the lads down and I had to think of the team. I suppose you could compare it to the FA Cup game years earlier but this had so much riding on it. We needed something from the match so the whole team had to be 100 per cent. For me, it was hell watching. It's a terrible feeling when you watch a game while injured and you cannot do anything about a result that will affect you and your career.

Again the Bristol City fans came out to support us. The gate was 38,000, which was incredible for us. Liverpool as always were full of internationals and on their way to the league title but yet again it was a fantastic performance from the lads. Gerry Sweeney, who was fast becoming a player who could play anywhere, did a great job at left-back, while Gerry Gow was excellent after coming back from a long-term injury.

But the star as per our other games was Chris Garland. We went 1-0 down after half an hour through Liverpool's David Johnson only for Chris to pull one back just before half-time with a diving header. In the second half Chris produced a bit of magic to put us 2-1 up. Ashton Gate was rocking and it reminded me of the night we beat Portsmouth to win promotion but I unfortunately felt a little detached from it all. We won 2-1 and it really did give us a lifeline in our fight to stay up. With other results coming in the bottom of the table had taken shape. Spurs were rock bottom along with Stoke. This meant a three-way shoot-out to avoid the dreaded third spot. We would be playing relegation rivals Coventry away, needing a point to stay up, while Sunderland, our other rivals, were at Everton and again just needing a point to avoid the drop.

We were, as you can imagine, all under pressure, but for me it was off the scale. I was so worried about Wendy and the twins that I really didn't know what to do, and with my injury too I was not in a great place emotionally. Before the Coventry game, Alan Dicks made the decision to leave me out of the team. I was so disappointed. I could have played but there was so much riding on this result that I just think Alan couldn't afford to take a chance on me. The lads rallied round, particularly Chris Garland as he knew what it meant to me. Here I was, the captain who had fought and pushed to get this team into the top flight and it all hinged on one game that I would watch from the stands.

I was on the floor in terms of my mood. I couldn't even bring myself to travel up to Coventry with the team as I just did not feel part of things, although looking back maybe I should have but as I said I was all over the place and instead I went up with Bristol City's assistant secretary John Lillington in his car. I remember all the fans going up the motorway with scarves and flags hanging out the windows. I saw the lads before kick-off and sat in the stand alongside John as one of the most bizarre games unfolded before us.

The game had been delayed by 15 minutes due to the size of the crowd. I'm not sure under whose instructions that was, but the delay would prove vital later on. Coventry tore into us from the off and went 1-0 up in the first half, then the second half exploded into life as Coventry went 2-0 up. I remember the sense of helplessness I felt as it looked like we were doomed despite what was happening between Everton and Sunderland. Suddenly we pulled one back with Gerry Gow and it seemed to give us the momentum and with ten minutes or so left Donnie Gillies popped up in the box to make it 2-2. With that, Coventry displayed on their electronic scoreboard that Sunderland had lost at Everton and at present ourselves and Coventry were safe. So with that the next ten minutes were taken up with players from both sides just passing the ball back to each other, happy to keep the game at 2-2.

The decision to delay the kick-off now seemed a perfect one but I'm sure if I was the Sunderland captain I would have been livid. The scenes at the end at Highfield Road were incredible as both sets of supporters ran on the pitch to congratulate both teams on staying up. I managed to fight my way through the throngs of fans and make my way down to the dressing room. When I saw the lads I was reminded of when I saw Keith Fear the night we won promotion against Portsmouth. He was pleased for us but he didn't seem part of it and that's how I felt. Sure, I drank champagne with my team-mates, but I wasn't on the pitch that night and it still hurts to this day. If I get in conversation with fans now and they ask me about the Coventry game they are really surprised that I never played and I have to admit it still rankles me today that I wasn't part of one of Bristol City's most famous nights, but I'm just so glad we got the result in the end.

So we were safe and taking stock, and if you look at our first season in the big time it certainly was an experience. There were things that I personally would have done differently and things I think the club should have done differently, but to have stayed in the division was a fantastic achievement for everybody connected with the club, even if it was down to the wire in the end.

9

Blue Skies and Black Clouds

I THINK it's safe to say that our first year in the big time was something of a rollercoaster for everybody connected with the club. The general feeling of relief seeped through Ashton Gate during the summer period but there was plenty of talk regarding why we struggled. Everyone had their own take on the season but mine was that I think we all knew that we were dealt such a blow in losing striker Paul Cheesley so early on, and although the signing of Chris Garland had in my opinion proved to be the thing that kept us up, we were all agreed that we did not want the forthcoming season to be that tight.

Outside of football, as a family we moved to Nailsea which was around three miles up the road from our previous home in Backwell. It was still in the countryside and still allowed me to continue with my love of all things farming.

As a team we were still optimistic for the new season but we were certainly brought back to earth in the first game when we lost 3-2 at home to Wolverhampton Wanderers. Things went from bad to worse as we couldn't get a win in our first five matches, losing three and drawing two. And as if things couldn't get any worse from a personal point of view, I then missed the next five matches through injury. To say I was disappointed was an understatement.

In my absence City had at least recorded their first win in the campaign, 3-2 over West Ham United at Ashton Gate. It was a decent performance and it was good to see youngster Kevin Mabbutt get on the scoresheet. Kevin had come through the youth ranks at City and like me he was an ex-England Schoolboys player who was much sought-after by bigger clubs than ourselves, but Kevin was a Bristol lad and his father Ray had played for rivals Rovers during the 1950s. Kevin was a really good player. He wasn't big like Paul Cheesley; he was more mobile and quick and had that striker's eye for goal which they all need. He was only 18 years of age so Alan Dicks knew he would not be the answer to our problem straight away, but given time he knew he could be.

Kevin was a really cool lad. We called him 'Socks' as he never wore any, and that fashion statement was something we all ended up following as even today I don't wear them, which is certainly cheaper for the family when it comes to Christmas presents. I liked Kevin a lot as he was always up with the latest trends and being a good-looking lad he was certainly popular with the ladies of Bristol. He drove a red Lotus Europa so he certainly looked the part as well. Kevin also had a manager or agent as it would be deemed today, and they set up a fan club and summer tours at schools where fans could meet him. We used to take the piss out of him for it but looking back he was somewhat ahead of his time in marketing himself as a footballer. To give him his due, all of this stuff he had going on never affected his performance on the field and in his first real season he did well for us.

One person who certainly helped Kevin in his football education and to be honest all of ours was Joe Royle. Joe arrived in the November of 1977 when we sat just above the relegation zone. He joined from Manchester City in a loan deal at first but signed permanently a few months later. Joe was a great man who had been there and done it all as a legendary centre-forward for Everton and England while also being a top professional at Manchester City. But to meet him, you would never know – he is such a down-to-earth guy who despite his amazing career never blew his own trumpet. He always gave advice and would rather listen to you about your career than talk about his own. He fitted into the dressing room perfectly and when he scored four goals against Middlesbrough at Ashton Gate on his debut, he had such a dry sense of humour that he just nonchalantly said, 'Well that's what I do every week,' which had the lads in stiches. I remember that game and I recall that when his third goal went in I had never seen a ball struck so hard in my life. Unfortunately for Joe, four goals on your debut is a bit of a millstone around your neck and he struggled to get into double figures for the rest of the season.

Another player who affected our campaign was centre-half Gary Collier. Gary was injured against Manchester United at Old Trafford. I remember the game being a real battle for me as I was in a constant tussle with United's centre-forward Joe Jordan, who was a handful at the best of times. It was an ill-tempered match with seven bookings but we came away with a 1-1 draw with Peter Cormack getting our goal. I can't remember Gary's injury specifically but it kept him out for the whole season.

With Gary out all the press were full of questions and theories over whether I would be making a return to the centre of defence alongside Norman Hunter. It may well have crossed my mind but Dave Rodgers, who was a great centre-half, did admirably in the role. I was now in a situation where I felt the club were up against it in terms of every season being a battle to stay up. It was such a transformation from the previous years where we were striving for this goal of being in the First Division. Now we were in the top flight and losing more, it meant the confidence throughout the team seemed to slowly fall away and I felt I never really had the influence on the lads that maybe I had in the past. I know it was never in my make-up to knock on Alan Dicks's door and demand that I was moved from the number three spot; I just felt that as long as I was in the team I could try and affect the club and my own future.

With us up against it in the league the only respite seemed to come from the Anglo-Scottish Cup, which we had entered on a few occasions. The competition had started in 1975, comprising of 16 teams from England and eight from Scotland. We all loved the tournament, especially the lads from north of the border, as it was a chance to go back up to Scotland and see family and friends. We used to travel by train and sometimes come home on the sleeper, not that there was much sleeping done on it as the lads would sit and play cards and generally have a laugh whatever the result. The games were a welcome change from the high pressure of the First Division and I seem to remember us beating rivals Bristol Rovers, Plymouth Argyle and Birmingham City before dispatching Partick Thistle home and way as well as Hibernian in what turned out to be a very competitive game over two legs. Norman Hunter and Peter Cormack were sent off at Easter Road and before the return leg at Ashton Gate the Hibs chairman dubbed us the 'butchers of Bristol'. We won the tie 6-4 on aggregate which meant a two-legged final against St Mirren, who were managed by a young Alex Ferguson. I don't really have any memories of Sir Alex as he has now become but I do remember him shouting and arguing with the officials during both games, so it certainly was a taste of things to come in his illustrious career.

We won the first leg 2-1 at Love Street with goals from Peter Cormack and Kevin Mabbutt, then drew the return at Ashton Gate 1-1 with a goal from Kevin in front of 17,000 fans. I know it wasn't the FA Cup or the League Cup but it was silverware and at that point in the season it seemed to give us a real boost as we ran around the pitch holding the cup aloft. As footballers you want to win competitions, and that's why I had real affection for the Anglo-Scottish Cup. I think it came at just the right time for us.

With the season coming into the business end we gained enough points at the start of 1978 to keep us up. It was just as well as we were awful in the run-in, winning only one of our last eight matches. We had improved on the previous season and finished 17th, just three points clear of West Ham, who went down along with Newcastle and Leicester.

With the campaign over it was great to get away with Wendy and the kids for a holiday. We chose the island of Sardinia and had a great time, getting away from the football. It was priceless being with the kids, swimming and playing on the beach. As any young family with children will tell you, when you travel you go with everything but the kitchen sink and this was no different for the Merricks as we enjoyed the Sardinian sunshine. As is typical for any dad, whether he is a footballer or not, he is left to carry all the bags like a pack horse and I was no different until during the holiday I picked up one of the bags and did not feel right at all. I had an excruciating pain in my groin area when I turned. I always kept myself fit on holiday and would go out a few mornings for a run but it was really painful. I knew this pain was worrying because as soon as I started to run again it just got worse. I tried not to let it affect our break but deep down I knew it would have to get sorted when I got back and pretty quickly if I was to start City's opening game away at newly promoted Bolton Wanderers.

When I came home I saw physio Les Bardsley and club doctor Mr Fowler. They could immediately see that I was in agony when I ran or twisted and turned, but the problem was they did not know why. I was then referred to a specialist who again had no idea as to the problem. The start of the season came and went for me and our versatile star Donnie Gillies was as usual doing a great job in my position, and although City were not pulling up any trees in the league they were at least holding their own, but it was a difficult time for me. I was happy the lads were doing okay but I on the other hand was out injured, unable to affect things on the pitch and injured with something that nobody could diagnose.

Added to this was rumblings within the club that maybe this mystery injury was just in my head. Whispers were about saying that 'he just doesn't want to play full-back' and 'he just don't want to play for us', or 'we all get pain, it must be in his head'. I had more meetings with specialists and another meeting with Dr Fowler. He was a lovely man but his advice was to go home and rest. He also told me a story of a lady who had a pain in her leg which became increasingly bad for her. So she persuaded the doctors to cut the leg off and yet the pain was still with her. The moral of the story was that the pain was in her own head and I then realised that this was the view of some people at the club.

Looking back, I understand his advice but mentally for me it was the last thing I needed. I knew I couldn't train with the lads but I just had to be at home. It was as though I was on lockdown. My mental state at this time was all over the place as I worried about my future in the game along with how I was going to pay the mortgage and feed my family. Bristol City were carrying on without me and I was just left alone at home with my thoughts, gradually going deeper into what I now realise was a state of depression.

I had to get out despite the injury. I did not tell the club but I contacted my friends Rex and Joe Baker, who ran the farm where I helped out, and they told me to come up and do a bit of work with them. I told them about my injury and that I would be taking it easy but it was more about being out in the fresh air and having human contact with people. Concentrating on animals that needed feeding along with fences that needed repairing stopped me from thinking about my future, which I believed was going to be one without football in it. I don't say lightly that I truly believed I was going to have to give up the game due to this injury. There was no light at the end of the tunnel for me as far as I could see.

Things just carried on with nobody looking for a cure and me just stuck injured away from the club. It didn't help that there were questions asked in the press about whether I was finished as a player. I don't blame the press as I was out of the side and nobody could tell them why or when I might return. I was very depressed by the whole situation and didn't know where to turn. Times like that make you realise how important your family and friends are to you. Wendy was incredible as were Rex and Joe at the farm; they will never know how important that place was to me at that time.

As the black cloud stayed over the Merrick household, a shining light appeared in the form of a phone call to my Nailsea home. I was pottering around the house trying not to get in Wendy's way and still very much in pain when walking when I answered the phone. A voice said, 'Hello, is that Geoff Merrick?' I replied yes and the caller said, 'This is Mike Summerbee.' I had played against Mike a few times and he is a fantastic bloke on and off the field and a legend for Manchester City. At the time he was coming to the end of his illustrious career and was playing for Stockport County. He went on, 'I bumped into Tony Collins and he said you were not playing due to a mystery injury. It sounds to me mate that you have exactly what I had a few years ago.' I couldn't believe it; this was so emotional for me to hear somebody actually say that they had the same injury and they had come through it. Those words meant the world to me and I was elated; my mood changed in an instant. I thought I could prove to people that it was not in my head after all.

I asked Mike what the problem was and he told me that it was called symptis pubis dysfunction, which is common in pregnant women. It's where your ligaments that keep your pelvis aligned become too slack. He also said that he made a point of telling Tony Collins that I would be back after treatment. Mike gave me a number for the specialist he had used in Manchester and told me the treatment was really painful but worth it, so I told him I would try anything as long as it meant I could kick a football again.

I came off the phone like a new man as I quickly explained to Wendy what Mike had said, and she was just as thrilled as me as she had seen what I had been going through. I then contacted the specialist to book the appointment. I also made the club aware but I still felt there was an element of scepticism towards the treatment in their view, although I didn't really care. I booked an initial consultation with the consultant, Freddie Griffiths, up in

Manchester. I couldn't drive due to the pain so I went up with my friend and City employee John Lillington. Mr Griffiths had worked with various sports stars and he confirmed everything Mike had said, also adding that the injury was particularly rare in footballers. He told me, as Mike had, that it would be painful as my symptis pubis needed repairing.

My next trip was days later. Again, John drove me up, and we stayed overnight as my appointment was first thing the following morning. The procedure meant that I was laid down and I had two injections under what I can only describe as my bollocks. The needle was massive and I originally thought that I was going to be knocked out for the procedure, but they needed me awake so I could tell them where the pain was. Well I could easily tell them the pain at the present time was under my bollocks where this massive injection had gone. After the procedure, I rested in the clinic before I went home. Mr Griffiths told me it would still be painful and it wasn't a miracle cure but after a few days I would certainly be feeling some improvement.

And that was what happened. I returned to the club and worked with the physios to stretch my abductor muscles, which are situated around your pelvis. It was the start of a stretching regime that I carried on throughout my career, even when I was playing non-league football. It was just something I had to get through to play. The club were pleased, as were my team-mates, especially as I was now back at training although it was early steps and I was a long way from being anywhere near the first team. My aim was to try and get in some friendly games when the season had finished and this I did, playing against Hungerford Town, Torquay United and Yeovil Town in May 1979. I can't tell you how great it felt to pull on the shirt again and actually kick a ball without pain; it really felt that there was light at the end of the tunnel for me.

As far as the first team were concerned, I had missed the whole season but to their credit they had finished 13th in the league which was a tremendous performance. The club were also now captained by midfielder Gerry Gow and I was okay with it; after all, I was concentrating on saving my career and not worrying over whether I was still captain, although it was a position I was incredibly proud of. Gerry was a completely different captain to me as he would shout and be very vocal on the field throughout a game whereas my style was to be a bit more arm round the shoulder towards players if they were having a tough time.

After the various friendlies the club had played, they were now ready to embark on a tour of North America. It was exciting for everyone and I was incredibly grateful that Alan Dicks chose to take me on the trip. Football, or soccer as it is known across the water, was just starting to take off in the United States with many British players playing for US and Canadian clubs during the summer. City were going to be playing four games on the tour and all the sides were a decent standard. I had not played or been involved in the first team for a whole season yet I think Alan felt it would do all of us good to try and get back to some sort of normality. It certainly did me the world of good emotionally to be back with the lads and feeling part of things, although when we arrived in Seattle after our long flight I started to worry again as I couldn't move because the pain had come back. I kept it to myself but I did tell Les Bardsley and Alan, who were supportive but I just couldn't believe that this could be happening all over again.

Our first game was against Seattle Sounders, whose team was managed by ex-Southampton star Jimmy Gabriel and contained players such as Alan Hudson, Mike England, Ron Davies and Bobby Howe. Les got talking to their medical team about my problem and they immediately organised for me to see their doctor, who instantly diagnosed the problem as Mr Griffiths had back in Manchester. Again I was given injections around the groin, which were just as painful, and told to stretch the abductor muscles, which I did. Although I didn't play due to the injury the tour was a success for the club, even though we lost that opening game. We then beat Vancouver Island and Portland Timbers while drawing with Vancouver Whitecaps.

On a personal note it was great to feel that I was back in the swing of things. I could feel the injury healing with every day that passed and as long as I continued my stretching regime I felt stronger and stronger. The season had been a nightmare for me. There were some very dark periods when I thought I was going to have to give the game up and thankfully now I was gearing myself up for another year in the top flight. Little did I know that the next season would be one of my best on a personal note but dreadful in terms of the team.

10

Changing Times

I SPENT the summer of 1979 working really hard on my fitness to be ready for another season in the top flight. My injury was clearing with every run and short sprint I did, but my only worry was whether I would be selected to play. Gerry Gow was now captain and I would be lying if I said I didn't miss the role, but you can't have a captain who can't get in the side because of injuries.

The previous season had been a nightmare for me both physically and emotionally, and I was glad to see the back of it. When we arrived back at Ashton Gate for 1979/80, changes were starting to happen. Alan Dicks had just splashed out £250,000, which was a club record, on striker Tony Fitzpatrick from St Mirren. Tony was a great lad who had impressed Alan during the clubs' Anglo-Scottish Cup matches but there was a real responsibility on him, especially as he had never played in the English league before.

As for departures, there were two massive bombshells on the horizon. The first was the exit of Norman Hunter. There had been rumours all summer that Norman would be leaving and I remember walking into the ground one morning and he pulled me to one side and told me he was going. He had been offered a player-coach role at Barnsley with his old team-mate Allan Clarke, who had just been installed as manager at Oakwell. It was a great move for Norman and his family but he was going to be a great loss to us.

I think over the years many fans feel that I would have been happy with Norman's departure as it freed up my number six shirt, but that was never the case. I liked Norman. He was great for us and gave his heart and soul to Bristol City, so I feared for the club as I knew what a loss he would be. I also had no divine right to be the new number six. Looking back, I don't know whether I would have done a better job than Norman over the years anyway.

The other bombshell was the departure of centre-half Gary Collier. Gary was a really talented and cultured footballer who had everything. He had come through the youth ranks and he had been coveted by many clubs over the years. Gary moved due to freedom of contract in what was a groundbreaking case. Before his fight in the courts, clubs held all the cards when it came to players' contracts. Gary had turned down City's offer of a new one and although this now put him on a weekly contract, the club did not want to negotiate a new one until the end of the season. That did not suit Gary so he fought his case to negotiate his own contract with other clubs. He won the case and a ruling was brought in that if players were out of contract they were free to talk to other clubs.

City had originally wanted £500,000 for Gary but a tribunal set the price at £325,000. Alan Dicks and the club were fuming at the result but a lot of the lads, me included, were pleased for Gary as we all knew the system at the time was very one-way and very much in favour of the clubs, but again it left us really vulnerable in a key area. I spoke with Gary at length and I feel he valued my opinion on and off the pitch. I was straight with him and told him that in my opinion he had chosen the wrong club. No disrespect to Coventry City but I thought he could have gone to a bigger club, and he would be reunited with John Sillett who was coaching at Highfield Road after joining from Hereford United. I didn't think John would get the best out of Gary. John was the type of guy who would shout and scream while working players hard, which there's nothing wrong with necessarily as it works for some, but Gary was the sort of person who responded to an arm round the shoulder. When we played with each other, if he made a mistake we would talk about it rather than shout at each other and he always responded to that type of approach.

Gary did well at Coventry City but never really reached the heights he should have and eventually joined Portland Timbers in the USA. I still speak to him now and again and he is loving life in the States with his family.

The whole affair sent a massive shock through the club, leading to Alan Dicks deciding that City were never going to be put in that position again. He and the board decided that certain players would be given long contracts to put off any club that came in for them. In hindsight it was a terrible decision as it was certainly going to affect the club in later years. Clive Whitehead was offered an 11-year deal, while Gerry Gow and Tom Ritchie were offered seven years. I was still on my usual contract, one year with a further year's option owned by the club, so it was essentially a two-year deal – so long as they took the option up. It was the sort of contract I had always had throughout my career.

There were no discussions in the dressing room about our various contracts – we just seemed to get on with things. If we were asked then we would be honest, and there was the usual banter regarding contracts, especially with the lads telling Clive that he would still be at City as a pensioner. I think Alan and the board were a bit naive as nobody thought about the bigger picture in terms of the club and what affect this would have. You have to remember that these contracts were offered, they were not thrashed out with the players' agents like today. They were just given, and who wouldn't want long-term security for their family?

The pre-season of 1979 really set the tone for what would be a football club that was about to spiral out of control, and for me it was a season that changed my life – not for the better. I have said many times in this book that I felt we were up against it during our time in the First Division, and this was never more prominent than this season. In our first four games we lost three and drew one, and although I was back with the number six shirt partnering Dave Rodgers in defence I was dropped for the next game at home to Ipswich Town. I wasn't happy and said a few things to Alan Dicks and reporter Peter Godsiff, then Alan came back in the paper and said he was going to sell me. He wasn't happy and I think it was a case of pure frustration on both our parts. We made up, I was fined and then I returned two weeks later for an away 0-0 draw at Nottingham Forest. Alan and I clashed no more than any experienced player and his manager would but we did have a mutual respect for each other and I always felt, like all the players, that we could voice our opinions. I think in this case he took exception to me talking to the press about our form.

The season just went from bad to worse and we were a club with no confidence whatsoever. As with winning, losing can also become a habit and that's what happened to us. When we had been in that position in our first season we had a spark that kept us going and unfortunately, although the players gave 100 per cent in every game, that spark just wasn't there this time around. Our fate was sealed by a 5-2 defeat away at Southampton, although I think everybody knew what was going to happen long before that game in April mathematically sent us down. We finished four points from safety and went down with Bolton Wanderers and Derby County.

Relegation is the most terrible thing for a player. You feel a failure and you really have to rely on your friends and family to pull you through it. I felt I had let the fans, all the staff at the club, and myself and family down. It consumed me. I have never really analysed what went wrong but I think there were many factors; the loss of key players like Paul Cheesley, Norman Hunter and Gary Collier and even my own injuries didn't help. We were just not good enough and although people have said City should have made signings when they were strong and maybe Alan was too loyal to us all, I also think the board never really dreamed we were going to stay in the top flight for four years and they found it difficult to cope in terms of planning and finance. It did make me laugh when they immediately took our £50 bonus away yet gave Alan a four-year deal. I'm sure the debate about why we went down still continues.

Added to all this was the fact I was named supporters' player of the year, which I was incredibly honoured by, especially as in certain parts of the club I had been written off the season before. I was apprehensive going to the awards night but the fans were brilliant towards me and their reaction to relegation appeared to be one of 'it was fun while it lasted' and there was always the next season to look forward to.

I had been busy off the pitch all season as well as this season was my testimonial year. I was originally going to have it the season before but physio Les Bardsley announced his retirement, so Alan asked me to move mine back. The testimonial is a thing of the past as the modern footballer does not really need the extra money it can bring, but back then it was a reward for long service. I really struggled with the concept of it and although I was grateful to the board that they acknowledged my 12 years' service to the club, going out organising dinners and trying to get sponsors and various companies to put their hand in their pocket and essentially give money to me was really difficult.

I was never happy doing speeches and being centre of attention but over the course of the year we had some great events. One of the guest speakers at a lunch was Wolverhampton Wanderers and Northern Ireland forward Derek Dougan. Derek was a smashing bloke and organised my testimonial match at the end of the season. Yet again fate dealt us a blow when the *Bristol Evening Post* went on strike, so it was difficult to promote the game, but my mate Barry Wyn hit on the idea of hooking up two speakers and a megaphone to my car and we both drove around south Bristol telling people to come to the game. That's laughable when you look back at it, but it was great fun.

The game was on 12 May, on a lovely warm Monday night. Relegation was still a cloud that hung over the club but 1,500 City fans came out to see the match and I thank every one of them for coming out and spending their money to support me. The match was a full Bristol City team against a Derek Dougan XI which included Peter Osgood, Norman Hunter, Cyrille Regis, Peter Barnes, Terry Cooper and John Wile. I was grateful to them all for turning out as we won 3-1.

Over the course of the fundraising season I had raised £8,000, which was incredible. The first thing I did was buy a car, and as I now had a growing family I bought a VW Passat estate.

After we had been relegated, the sponsor took the Scirocco off me – rubbing more salt in the wound. I went away with the family in the summer of 1980 and that combined with some trips to the farm helped me in some way to overcome the disappointment of relegation. I don't think deep down anybody thought we would come straight back up, and as far as I was concerned I just wanted us to stabilise things but that didn't happen.

Various players left and I understood that money would be tight for the club after relegation. Joe Royle went to Norwich City while Donnie Gillies crossed Bristol to join Rovers, and as per usual the departures weakened the strength of the side on and off the pitch. There was the usual paper talk regarding money troubles and also it was rumoured that the club would take any offers on us as players but as a team we didn't really believe it and our main concern was trying to get us challenging at least for promotion.

Although pre-season was good, our start to the season was dreadful as we couldn't get a win in our first four games, including a dour 0-0 at home against Rovers, who were now in our division. The fans were not happy and gates dropped due to a combination of relegation and being in the Second Division. I really can't put my finger on why we were struggling so much. We should have been up near the top as the players had not become bad overnight. Maybe we just struggled to come to terms with the Second Division.

Things came to a head after a 1-0 defeat at home to Swansea City. The fans turned on chairman Leslie Kew and manager Alan

Dicks, and the outcome was that Alan was sacked. It was the end of an era. A lot of the players, like myself, who had been on this fantastic journey with Alan, felt for him and also there was an element of responsibility on our part but I think the board and Alan knew deep down that he had run his course and the club needed fresh impetus. I would love to say that Alan came and gave us a rousing speech before he left but that was not the case – he just slipped away, which was a shame. He had been at Bristol City for around 14 years and had done something that no City manager to date had done by taking the Robins into the top flight.

Alan's assistant Tony Collins and coach Ken Wimshurst, a former City player, were put in charge until a replacement could be found. The results went from bad to worse as we lost our next three games, which was no reflection on Ken and Tony, but we were on the floor in terms of confidence and needed a boost that they just couldn't provide. Rumours were rife as to who would be coming in, and there was even talk that I might step up but I never saw myself as a manager, although I enjoyed coaching later in life. The strong favourite was Norman Hunter, who was still at Barnsley and doing a really good job. Norman was popular with the players and would have been a brilliant appointment and given the squad and the fans a real lift, but it was not to be as he apparently turned the club's offer down.

So, in the October, our new manager along with his assistant walked through the door: Bob Houghton and Roy Hodgson. As a group of players we were very much underwhelmed as we had not heard of them before. Bob had played non-league football for Hastings United and had coached abroad. He really made his name in Sweden where he took Malmö to the 1979 European Cup Final before being beaten by Brian Clough's Nottingham Forest. He arrived at City after a spell at Ethnikos Piraeus in Greece. His assistant Roy had played non-league football with Gravesend & Northfleet and had also coached in Sweden, where he met Bob.

There is always an element of fear in players when a new manager arrives. Players are worried that they may not be the manager's cup of tea or they give an extra ten per cent in training to try to impress, but for us it was just bewilderment about the appointment. Both men came in and were around the same age as me and they just appeared really flash and aloof towards the players. I know things had to change but they gave the impression that they were modern coaches who were using the appointment merely as a stepping stone to bigger and better things. We gave them the benefit of the doubt as we all wanted to get the club back up the table but when it came to coaching, things were really different. Under Alan, we would run, play a lot of five-a-sides and do sprints while focusing on us as players. Bob was very keen on focusing on the opposition in terms of dossiers and analysis. We were also going to be playing a route-one style which was all about defence and getting the ball up to the forwards as quick as possible, bypassing the midfield. This was dreadful news for the likes of Clive Whitehead, Trevor Tainton and especially Gerry Gow, who just watched the ball go over their heads.

Our training was also different and I'm sure now it would be looked at as the norm in terms of modern football but back then we really did not have a clue how this would help us. We spent a lot of time in the gym working on weights and concentrating on improving individually. Bob and Roy also liked us to have a ball and do tricks such as keepy-uppies. I remember thinking 'I'm not in a circus' and I couldn't see how that was going to help me on a rainy night away against Carlisle United, but we just got on with things.

Houghton lost his first game, 1-0 away at Grimsby Town, although his home debut was a 2-1 win against Luton Town in front of only 7,500 fans. The dropping home attendances certainly sent a message out to the board and players that the supporters were now down to the hardcore support and full houses against the likes of Liverpool seemed a distant memory.

In the October, Gerry Gow left for Manchester City. Gerry was the heart and soul of the club and he became so frustrated with the way things had gone that he felt he had to move away. We spoke about the old days quite a lot and I wished him well. He was a massive loss for us in the dressing room and throughout the club. At the end of the month I was made captain due to Gerry's departure, which also coincided with my 400th game, at home to Derby County. It was a great day despite the 2-2 draw as I was also offered a new three-year contract worth £400 a week. It was the longest contract I had been given in my career and of course the most money. I signed it as I was happy at the club despite the freefalling through the divisions. I was around 30 years of age and playing well in what was a side low in confidence, and the contract also gave me a bit of financial security, so I had no desire to move away.

Results did not improve for us and things went from bad to worse in a November home game with Oldham Athletic. I went for a ball and got my foot stuck in the mud, then an Oldham player crashed into me and I spun round but my ankle stayed rooted to the turf and I heard a crack. The pain was terrible and I had broken my ankle. I was stretchered off and I never really thought about the enormity of the injury until I had an operation and was lying in the hospital. I thought to myself that it probably was going to be the end of my career and would be a long recovery.

I wasn't wrong and I was finished for the rest of the 1980/81 season. I kicked a few balls in training towards the end but I was nowhere near the first team and as far as Bob Houghton was concerned, I don't think he was that encouraging about me getting there anyway. I remember after one session he called me into his office and asked me about whether I had thought about retiring, as in his opinion I was finished. It really knocked my confidence but I told him I thought he was wrong and I would be back and ready for selection at some point.

The time in recuperation was a nightmare for me as City were relegated that season and although I had played 17 games, there was nothing worse than watching them fall down into the

Third Division while there was nothing I could do about it. The black clouds that hovered over the club showed no signs of lifting. But those clouds were nothing compared to what was round the corner for the club and me and my family.

11
Kicked Out of the Door

THE EVENTS of the 1981/82 season have continued to affect my life even today. The only way to describe what happened is that it was an event that devastated myself and my family and it's something that scarred me unimaginably. I also know I will carry around the hurt of before and after that period forever.

There have been many articles and stories about why the 'Ashton Gate Eight' were forced to tear up their contracts to save Bristol City. I know people are entitled to their opinion and I respect that, but not everybody is aware of all the facts. This section of the book was always going to be a hot topic in terms of my own thoughts and as I said to Neil, I will talk about it now, get it out there and probably never mention it ever again. It was a bolt from the blue and it was certainly something that I could not prepare for.

We started the season off the back of a Swedish tour. We played four games and won them all; I don't think we even conceded a goal in the matches so spirits were high but things were certainly different under Bob Houghton as we were all expected to be in bed at 10.30pm. That would never have happened in F-Troop's day but it was a new regime and even though it did not fill us players with any great confidence in our management team we just got on with things and looked toward the coming season.

After some friendlies at home against the likes of Torquay United, Crystal Palace and Charlton Athletic, we set ourselves up and were ready for a new season in the Third Division. We were all positive and thinking that maybe we could stop the rot and at least make things stable. The personnel in the dressing room was starting to change as Bob tried to bring in his own players. We had the likes of Jan Möller, who had signed from Bob's previous club, Malmö, for £120,000. Jan was a big Swedish goalkeeper who settled in with the lads well. We also signed powerful centre-forward Mick Harford from Newcastle United for £160,000. Mick was a no-nonsense striker who was great in the air and took no prisoners. He fitted the footballing DNA of Bob and Roy perfectly as it was a case of getting the ball up to Mick as quickly as possible. Added to these lads were a few youngsters as well as people such as myself, Trevor Tainton, Kevin Mabbutt, Gerry Sweeney, Jimmy Mann and Dave Rodgers.

We opened our campaign away at Carlisle United with a 2-2 draw. Another draw at home to Doncaster Rovers followed before an away defeat at Fulham. We had also been drawn against Walsall in the League Cup, which was over two legs. We won the first leg 2-0 at Ashton Gate thanks to goals from Mick Harford and Jimmy Mann. But we lost 1-0 in the return game, a night I remember as I pulled a hamstring after stretching for the ball. I was playing well at the time so I was gutted as it meant I would be out for some time, and little did I know that it would be my last competitive game in the red shirt of Bristol City.

I knew the recovery of the injury was going to be long and one thing was for sure, I had the mental toughness to get over an injury as I had showed many times before. The problem was my confidence was not matched by Bob Houghton, who yet again pulled me to one side at our training ground in the Stockwood area of Bristol and told me that he thought I was finished. I just told him the same as I had done the last time he mentioned it – that I would be back for selection soon.

In the October, City swapped Kevin Mabbutt for £100,000 and Crystal Palace midfielder Terry Boyle. They also sold Clive Whitehead to West Bromwich Albion for £100,000, stating that there were problems financially as the club were losing money on a weekly basis. You did not have to be a genius to know that consecutive relegations and dwindling crowds would put pressure on the directors but as players we never knew the half of what was going on behind the scenes.

Results failed to improve and we were freefalling to the bottom of the Third Division. After a 3-1 home defeat to Wimbledon, Bob was relieved of his duties and his assistant Roy Hodgson took over. I felt sorry for Bob even though we never really saw eye to eye regarding tactics and training. He was a decent man and it was no fun when anybody lost their job. Roy was a good bloke also but the two of them were just the wrong type of manager for us at that time. We needed somebody who was going to try and regenerate the spirit that we had always had, yet it had gone desperately missing in the last couple of seasons.

I would love to be able to tell you what things were like under Roy's managership but unfortunately I never got the chance to find out. The date was 23 January 1982, and 21 days since Houghton's departure. I was returning to Ashton Gate after playing a morning game in the reserves at Arsenal. I had played well and my hamstring had cleared up with no ill effects, so I was ready for selection for the first team. They had just been beaten 1-0 at home by Aston Villa in the FA Cup. When I got to Ashton Gate the crowd was drifting away and the players were getting changed. We were chatting about the games we had just played in and although the lads were disappointed, they had still done well against a strong Villa side.

With that, midfielder Jimmy Mann came into the dressing room and gave us a tiny, ripped-up bit of paper from a notebook. On it were seven names: Geoff Merrick, Trevor Tainton, David Rodgers, Chris Garland, Julian Marshall, Peter Aitken, and his own. It had been given to Jimmy by one of the directors with the instructions that we were all to meet the following day in the boardroom. That one act set the tone for what was to come and how we as players were going to be treated. It was also a good indicator of how we were viewed by the directors at the time. They gave Jimmy a scrap of paper, not official letters to us from the club outlining their plans. They wanted to ambush us, and the directors never had the decency, respect or guts to speak to us individually to tell us about the meeting and its content. It was a cowardly act on their part and set the tone for what was to come.

Nobody had a clue as to what the meeting was about and I mulled over it with Wendy when I got home, but I still had no clue. We all arrived at Ashton Gate still clueless as to why we were there, and were then joined by an eighth player in the shape of Gerry Sweeney, who had been told to come to the club immediately. He said he was at home washing his car at the time and was still in his Bristol City tracksuit, which prompted Chris Garland to say that Gerry was going to be the new manager, but he could not have been further from the truth.

We walked into the boardroom and were met by some board members and the chairman Archie Gooch. He introduced the club's accountant, a man called Chris Barlow. Gooch and Barlow came straight to the point and told us that the club had debts of around £900,000, a figure which was rising by the week. They explained that two local businessmen, Deryn Collier and Ken Sage, would raise £1m in shares and had put together a proposal where the club needed to go into liquidation while still paying HMRC and the bank. They would then form a new company called Bristol City 1982 and that would see the rebirth of the club and in the future make it a better prospect for potential buyers.

In order for that to happen, they wanted us all to rip up our contracts to save the club. We were stunned and just looked at

Luckwell school team with me holding the ball

Captain of England Schoolboys, introducing the right honorable Horace Thomas before the England v West Germany game at Wembley in 1966

Me introducing the dignitaries to my team-mates before the England v Wales Schoolboy International at Ashton Gate

My England Schoolboy cap hanging up at the farm

My England Schoolboy shirt on display at the farm

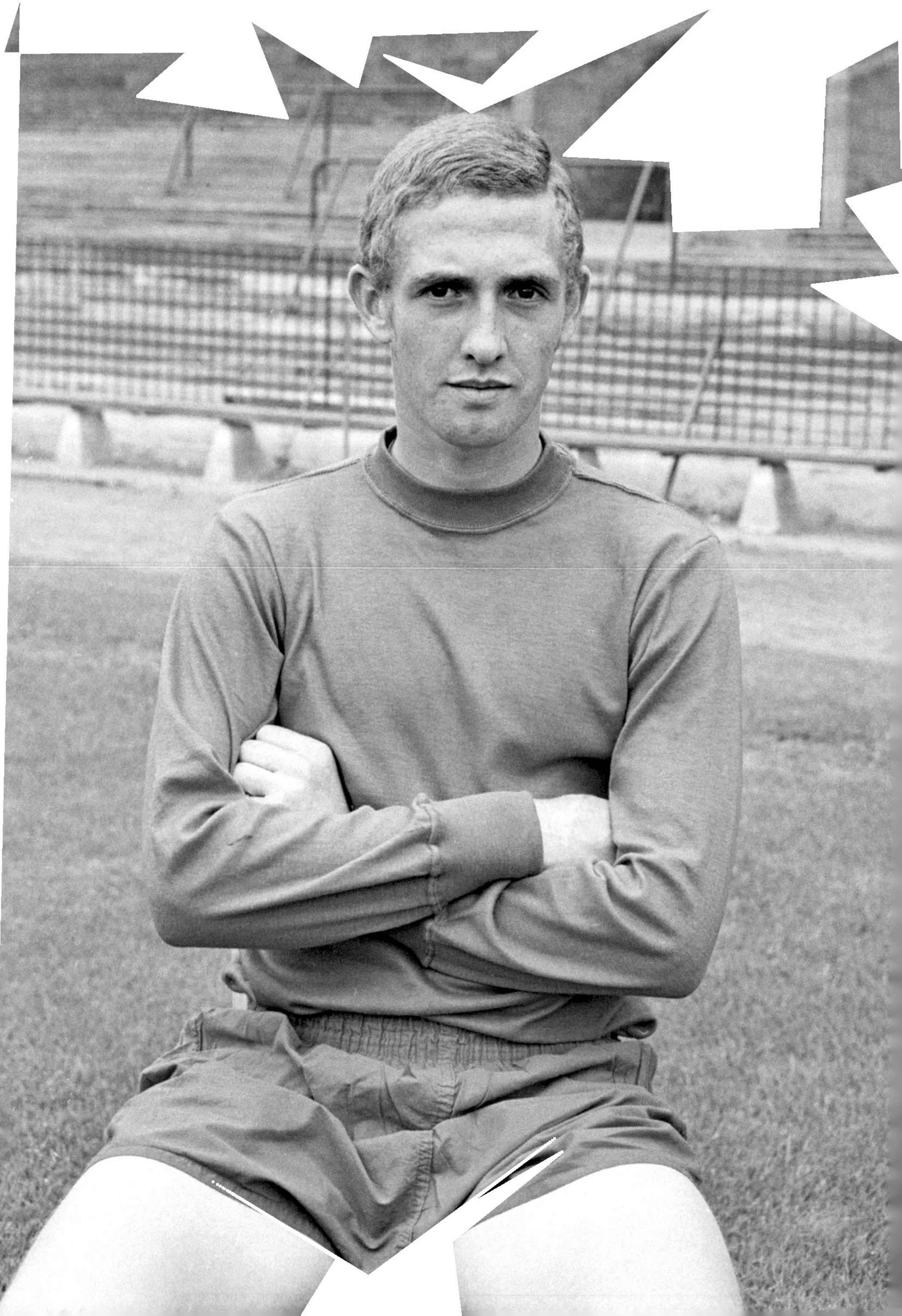

Me around the 1973/74 season

I celebrate a rare Merrick goal

Another leap as I tangle with Crystal Palace midfielder Steve Kember at Ashton Gate

Another day's graft on the farm

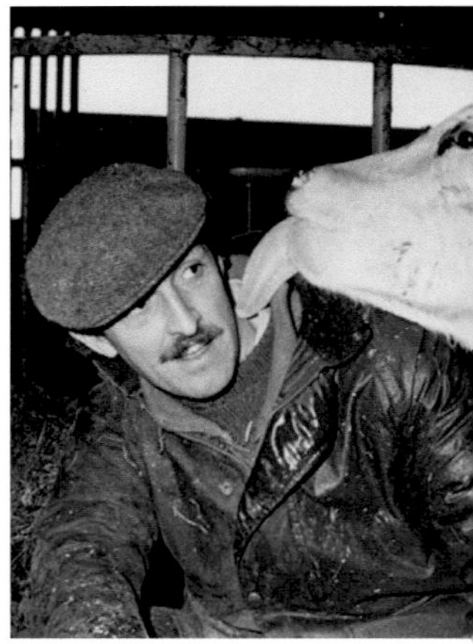

A fan on the farm

Presentation with from left to right: Paul Cheesley, Gerry Gow, Frankie Prince of Bristol Rovers, Me, Bryan Drysdale

The arrival of the beard

Some of the Bristol City players and staff with their wives at an awards dinner in Bristol

Promotion to the big time

Me with my friend and author Neil Palmer holding my promotion shirt from the 1975/76 season

A Bristol City photo opportunity with the girls from club sponsor Perma Shine

Bristol City 1976/77 squad. (Back row, from left) Donnie Gillies, Ray Cashley, John Shaw and Clive Whitehead, (middle row, from left) Alan Dicks (manager), Paul Cheesley, David Rodgers, Tom Ritchie, Gary Collier, Ken Wilmhurst (coach) and Les Bardsley (physio), (front row, from left) Michael Brolly, Jimmy Mann, Brian Drysdale, Geoff Merrick, Trevor Tainton, Gerry Sweeney and Gerry Gow.

In pursuit of George Armstrong in the Robins' First Division debut at Highbury

With Alan Dicks in the City dugout at training

Away at Birmingham City in one of my favourite City kits

Bristol City in 1978. Left to right Back Row: Peter Cormack, John Shaw, Clive Whitehead, Ray Cashley, Howard Pritchard. Middle Row: Tony Collins, Norman Hunter, Tom Ritchie, Dave Rodgers, Gary Collier, Joe Royle, Alan Hay, Ken Wimshurst. Front Row: Kevin Mabbutt, Jimmy Mann, Trevor Tainton, Alan Dicks, Geoff Merrick, Gerry Sweeney, Donnie Gillies

Me, Wendy and Charlie enjoying the countryside

With Derek Dougan at my Testimonial Dinner

The Ashton Gate Eight await their fate in a Bristol hotel. From left to right, standing: Me, Jimmy Mann, Julian Marshall. Seated: Left To Right: Chris Garland. Gerry Sweeney, Peter Aitken, Trevor Tainton, Dave Rodgers

Me (number 20) jumping with Caroline Hill team-mate goalkeeper Tony Kiefer in a match against South China at the Hong Kong Stadium, April 1982

At home with the Merricks: Me, Wendy, Charlie with twins Elliott (left) and Luke behind

Life on the buildings

Wendy (left) and my dear friend Marina Dolman

Boys and their toys

Relaxing at home with Bert, the best dog in the world

each other. They had clearly prepared everything but this news was like a punch in the stomach. I remember mumbling out a few words like, 'When will this happen?' Gooch replied, very self-assuredly, 'By the end of the week. We will sort any money matters you might have after that.' The whole board seemed very businesslike and the fact that we were still processing this news meant that I'm sure they thought everything was going to plan. When we did get ourselves together mentally, we told them that this was a disgrace and I said that we needed the Professional Footballers' Association involved and there was no way that this would be done and sorted in a week as we would fight it. The atmosphere in the room was dreadful, everyone was having their say and things were said by directors about certain players' careers that were unforgivable. From our point of view there was no respect for us either as players or men. The board had no empathy for us and showed us very little regard towards what we would be giving up. It was as if our careers at the club had counted for nothing, which was hard to take, particularly when they referred to us as non-essential creditors of the club. The meeting ended in an incredibly hostile way so we organised another one, this time at the Dragonara Hotel in Bristol, where we would be represented by our union.

We just walked out of Ashton Gate in a daze. We said a few words to each other and made our way home to tell our families. I don't remember my drive home but I'm sure I was in shock all the way. The club then informed the *Bristol Evening Post* and

Western Daily Press, and various local TV companies, about their plans. That's when the pressure started. When I got home and told Wendy we ended up in tears, with the kids just looking at us. Charlie was now nine so she understood what was happening; the twins were five but they could see we were upset even though we tried to hide it from them. I just felt absolute panic and fear as to what the future would hold for us. We never lived an extravagant lifestyle and had a normal house with a mortgage, which I was now worrying about paying. I couldn't believe that after all these years Bristol City did not want me any more.

My mind was all over the place and in among all this I started to get calls from journalists asking if it was true that the club was in the players' hands. This was the line that the club spun to the public and the press, that we were on massive money and really long contracts, and were the reason for the perilous financial state. This was simply not true.

Days later the press even published pictures of our houses with the article stating that they were where the money had gone. There was also an article about all the staff at Ashton Gate, in which they stated that they hoped the players would do the right thing and help them keep their jobs, and as you can imagine the pressure was enormous. We were also subjected to death threats and phone calls at all hours of the day and night telling us that we needed to rip up our contracts to save the club. Wendy was followed everywhere, as I was, with people shouting for us to do the right thing. This was the same for all the players at that time.

Businessman Deryn Collier spoke to a mutual friend of ours who then turned up at my house unexpectedly to tell me that I had to make sure the lads all gave up their contracts. I know people talk about mental health more freely today than years ago but mine at that time was in such a low and dark place that I didn't think I would ever recover. I spoke to Gordon Taylor, the chairman of the PFA, and he agreed to come down to Bristol to fight our cause, although he openly admitted he had never heard anything like what was being asked of us in all his time in football.

During this time I received a call at home from a guy called Trevor Joiner. Trevor was the owner of the Cadbury Court Country Club outside Bristol, a popular haunt for many of the City lads back in the day. Trevor told me about a member, David Bird, who was an accountant with offices in Bristol, and I should ring him as he wanted to help. I phoned David straight away and he told me that in his opinion what he was hearing was a disgrace. He thought we were being shafted and that there was still a way that the club could carry on with the debt and keep the players. He also said he would offer his services for free. I was overwhelmed as throughout this nobody had said they wanted to help us.

David said he had worked on a proposal which he felt would be better if it was headed up by the PFA. I contacted them and we went up to their base in Manchester to meet their management committee to talk about the idea, but incredibly they never wanted to pursue it. After trying to get them to change their mind with no success, we left Manchester inconsolable. We could not believe that they were not interested; they just wanted to negotiate what Bristol City were offering so David's plan never saw the light of day.

David was a massive help to me during this terrible time. He would take me shooting in the countryside and we just talked and walked, which helped me take my mind off things, even for a few hours. As a group we met up again for another round of meetings with Gordon Taylor negotiating with us. Our first offer from the board was for £50,000 split between the eight of us, which would mean £6,250 each. We all agreed that it was a pittance. My contract had one year and ten months to run and it was worth £35,500, along with a £10,000 loyalty bonus if I reached so many games over 400, which I and some of the lads had done. All our contracts were around the same and in total they were worth £280,000. The offer was rejected and the club came back with £86,000, again split among us at £10,750 each. Once again it was rejected by us.

We ended the meeting and arranged to meet on the morning of Tuesday, 3 February at the Dragonara Hotel. It would be a date never to be forgotten. We met up in our usual hotel suite but this time there was a midday deadline set by the club's receivers. We were instructed that if we could not agree the terms offered then there was no bluffing, the club would definitely fold at one minute past 12. The feelings within the room were of anger, sadness, fear and despair. I noticed a young woman with another guy and they did not seem that interested in the proceedings so I asked Gordon Taylor who they were and he just said they were friends of one of the PFA assistants. I went mad and told him to get them out. I said, 'Do you realise what this is all about? It's not a little get-together, this is our lives we're fighting for. The next couple of hours will define our futures and our families' futures. Get them out and let's sort this out.'

I had taken on the spokesman role among the players and as captain I was happy to do it, but I was at breaking point. As a group we sat together in this room and talked among ourselves about our futures and how any offer would impact on all our personal circumstances. The strain was unbearable as we awaited the club's next proposal. I can only compare it to somebody who is waiting for a jury's decision in court when they are innocent of a crime.

You could see that we were all shell-shocked by the events. I had been at the club for over 15 years, Trevor Tainton the same, Dave Rodgers 11 years, Chris Garland 12 years on and off, Gerry Sweeney 11 years, Jimmy Mann eight years and then you had Peter Aitken who had been at City for two years and Julian Marshall one year. We all had different personal and financial circumstances and we all had families who had to be looked after, so whatever was offered had to work for us. With an hour to go to the deadline the club gave us their final offer, £100,000 between the eight of us and the possibility of a testimonial at some point. That was the final offer, and if we still did not agree the club would fold. We knew there was nothing we could do; we had been beaten down mentally by the whole affair. In truth there was only really going to be one outcome and that was in favour of the club. The country's press were waiting outside for an outcome and all the City fans were listening intently to their radios eager for news as to whether the club would still be in existence.

The offer gave us £12,500 each, so the doors opened and the news was forwarded to the media, and more importantly the board were informed of our decision to accept. My career at Ashton Gate was over. As we made our way out of the hotel, through the scramble of press and TV men taking photos and wanting interviews, I just felt hurt, anger and sadness. It was the end of my relationship with the club that I loved dearly and could have left many times in my career but chose to stay loyal to as I never wanted to play for anybody else. The whole experience broke my heart and broke my mind.

I thought about when Fred Ford came to my house to sign me and all those great players I had looked up to and played with during my career. In total I had played 427 games and scored 13 goals for Bristol City. On reflection, I was so sad that I never got to say goodbye to the fans in a packed Ashton Gate as my last game in the ground was for the reserves with hardly anybody there to see it. That wasn't the way I wanted to finish my career at the club and I am not ashamed to say that when I got home and was among my family I cried. I was heartbroken as it all felt so unjust.

What was particularly upsetting was that since that day the directors who were involved in that shameful incident never once picked up the phone and asked if any of us were okay or if we needed anything. It's something that still rankles even now. I called this chapter 'Kicked Out of the Door' as that was how I felt. We were yesterday's news as far as the club were concerned as they now became Bristol City 1982. That's how I view them now, and for me they lost all the history that went before it when they took the club into receivership.

As the years have gone by we as players have always been known as the Ashton Gate Eight and I'm glad that people remember what we did, but I would not want that to define our careers. We were all very good players who had our own individual highs and lows at the club and gave everything for the red shirt, some of us for a long time and others all too briefly.

So looking back at that time you may well ask what my feelings are now. I know there are many opinions about the Ashton Gate Eight and I respect them all. People say things like, 'Everybody loses their job at some time.' I agree and I feel for anybody who goes through redundancy, but we are all different and we handle it in different ways. Nobody can really speak about my experience other than me. I think the saying is that you can't judge somebody until you have walked in their shoes, and I think that's very true of this case. People also say we were finished and nobody wanted to buy us, but my response to that is the club just wanted to get rid of us as soon as possible, hence the fact that they wanted us to go within the week so there was no time to sell us. As for being finished, we all ended up with clubs in the end; Trevor and Dave went to Torquay United, Julian ended up at Blackburn

Rovers, Jimmy signed for Barnsley and Gerry and Peter joined York City. As for Chris Garland he was like me and we both didn't have the stomach and we both had no desire to kick a ball again.

I know it's well documented also that the PFA were not at their best in helping us but to be honest I felt that it was all new to them. We all know it would never happen to players today so I hope the PFA learned a few lessons from our situation.

What really gets to me in this sad piece of Bristol City history is not only the lack of respect shown to us during and after this event but the way that the board spun the truth regarding their situation and mis-management of the club to the press and more importantly the fans. Even today I hear fans saying, 'Well the club went bust due to the Ashton Gate Eight being on big money and long contracts,' and that's not the case. By the time we ripped up our contracts the club were just over £1m in debt. Our existing deals were worth £280,000 combined. And all of the offers we received, there were no agents involved and long negotiations with us trying to screw the club over. The directors knew what they could afford at the time and that's what was offered to us.

The longest contract in place was Jimmy Mann's, which had two and a half years left, so these were hardly massively long deals compared to what was portrayed by the club. They put us up as the bad guys to cover their own mis-management. They still owed money to Malmö for the Jan Möller transfer, as well as being behind by £100,000 to Newcastle United for Mick Harford. The Dragonara Hotel was owed £6,000 and money was due to catering companies, pitch suppliers, coach companies, printers and drinks suppliers to name a few. And all those creditors could expect just 14p in the pound in return. All of this was not our fault yet we were gone and splashed all over the press and hounded to 'Do the Right Thing'.

In hindsight maybe I was too loyal and trusting towards the club. I know there were occasions where I put the club before my career and that is a regret I have. When things died down, I went to work as a labourer on my friend's farm and it did me the world of good. It cleared my mind, which was a slow process, but I needed rebuilding in terms of what I had been through. I had lost a stone in weight and my mind was badly scarred by the event. Being out of the spotlight and concentrating on earning money for us as a family to get by on, although hard, really helped me but I was never really the same again.

I wasn't really thinking about a possible return to football when out of the blue I got a call at home from a guy who represented a consortium of businessmen who owned a few clubs in Hong Kong. He told me he wanted myself and Jimmy Mann to go out there, initially for six months, and play for a team called Caroline Hill in the Hong Kong league. At first I thought it was a wind-up but the more detail he went into the more I realised it wasn't and financially it would be a good move, although it would mean being away from Wendy and the kids. I told him I was interested in principle but I would have to check with Wendy and Jimmy. Wendy was fine. She said she was going to miss me but knew the financial benefit of going. I contacted Jimmy and he was keen, so things were set in place for us to fly out in a couple of weeks.

Unfortunately Jimmy then got cold feet and pulled out, so I asked Chris Garland if he fancied it. Although at first apprehensive, Chris agreed so I contacted the businessmen and they were fine with Chris coming out instead. Then with days to go until we flew out I received a call from Norwich City boss Ken Brown asking whether I had been fixed up with a club but I told him I was going abroad, then my old pal Bobby Campbell got in touch. He was managing Portsmouth in the Third Division. Bobby asked if I was fixed up and if not, I should go down and play for him. I was 31 years old and he said he needed some experience in the side.

I told him I was going abroad and he asked where, so I told him it was Hong Kong and I would be playing for Caroline Hill. Bobby shouted, 'Jesus Christ, not them, I have just come back from managing them and it's bloody awful out there. Don't do it Geoff, it will be a bloody disaster.' I told him I gave the people in Hong Kong my word and couldn't go back on that. It was another example of me being too loyal to people; I gave my word and that was it. But Bobby wasn't entirely right, Hong Kong wasn't a disaster, although it was more of an experience never to be forgotten.

12
A Hong Kong Adventure

I THINK to an outsider it would be easy to think of my time in Hong Kong as a disaster. It certainly did not work out as Chris and I had hoped but it was, if anything, an adventure for both of us. The reality of the situation was that we just should not have gone. We were both damaged mentally by the whole Ashton Gate Eight affair and I know when I take stock of it all I feel as though I was just running away from that situation. The best move for me would have been to sign for a club here in the UK, but I felt that the break away from British football would do me good and would in some way help with the way I was feeling.

It was a crazy idea really; the thought that I should go thousands of miles away from my wife and kids to a foreign land and play for a club where I knew nobody and in some way that would make me feel better was crazy. The only good thing about it was that I was going with one of my best mates, who was feeling exactly the same as me.

When the day for us to fly off came round I really was heartbroken. The kids were at a friend's farm as a big goodbye with them would have been too painful for me. I remember looking at Wendy on our doorstep; she looked gorgeous as always whereas I had lost a stone in weight and was a mess. My friend Roger Smith, who was a big City fan, had offered to take me and Chris up to Heathrow in his Rolls-Royce of all things. Wendy and I talked until Roger pulled into our drive, and then we knew that was it. We embraced and off I got into the car. I know it wasn't as if I was going to war but for me and my family we were going through our own personal war which meant I had to go away, because I had given the people in Hong Kong my word.

We drove off and picked up Chris who, like me, had said had a very emotional goodbye to his wife Trish and their children. Once the tears were wiped away we set off up the M4 and although it sounds harsh we tried to focus on what lay ahead rather than think about our families. We arrived at Heathrow and said our goodbyes to Roger. Soon we were in the air and our 6,000-mile journey to Hong Kong had begun.

I am not a great believer in omens but we had to divert at one point to Calcutta in India as a passenger had died during the flight and the body had to be removed, with Calcutta being the nearest airport. We were both stunned; what a start for us. We got off the plane in India and walked round the airport until the plane was ready to continue some two or three hours later, although it did cross both our minds to get on the next flight back home. In the end we put those thoughts to the back of our minds and carried on with the trip.

Eventually we arrived in Hong Kong and after picking up our bags we walked towards the exit sign where we hoped our hosts would be waiting for us. Sure enough, in the arrivals area was a huge man with two pictures taken out of football magazines, of me and Chris. He greeted us and led us to a car. We drove through Hong Kong and it was amazing; although tired, we were like little kids as we pointed things out to each other and stared up at the huge tower blocks that circled the city. We were happy as up until then we had not even signed a contract with our hosts, so at least they had turned up. It was always in the back of my mind that they wouldn't.

We were not so happy when our driver took us to the club's hostel in the middle of the city. He explained in broken English that it was where we would stay.

We entered the building and it was a state; it was filthy with cockroaches and rats scurrying around. The dorms had bunk beds and there were players from the club all lying in their beds with various washing hung out on string across the room. It was also incredibly hot with no ventilation in the place. Now I know we were two lads from south Bristol and we could muck in with the best of people but we certainly were not expecting this. Chris, ever the diplomat, said, 'Bollocks to this, let's go home.' I explained that we couldn't as we had given them our word and as we had arrived we should try and sort something out. I told the driver that we were not staying there. He then spoke to somebody at the hostel and told us to get back in the car, before he proceeded to drive us across town to a very fashionable hotel in the city where we were to stay.

Looking back, I think the club just tried it on. They had a room booked for us in the hotel but wanted to see if we would stay there in the hostel and save themselves a few quid. It appeared that all the local players were staying in the hostel and all the players from overseas were in hotels or apartments across the city. When we eventually got to our room we settled down and I can remember it was without doubt the worst night's sleep I have ever had in my life. I tossed and turned all night and thought about Wendy and the kids, I tried to work out what the time at home was and what they would be doing, but all of this was just spinning in my head. They were on my mind right through until daybreak. The next morning was really hard but I knew I would have to put those thoughts to the back of my mind if the move was going to work out.

We were taken to see our new employers and meet the team. Caroline Hill Football Club were formed in the 1950s by auto shop workers. They had experienced a few highs during that time and now they were experiencing some lows as they were fighting at the bottom of the league. Football was popular in Hong Kong, mainly due to the British influence on the colony. It had really taken hold during the 1950s and remained popular. Caroline Hill were owned by a lady called Veronica Choo, who also owned a few other clubs in the league. It was an example of how different things were on this side of the world in terms of ownership. Our manager and coach was a large, military-style man who had to be all of 18st. His name was Chan Chung Yeung and his assistant was a former Peruvian international striker called Augusto Palacios, who had played and managed all over the world. Both gentlemen welcomed us warmly

Caroline Hill were almost two-thirds of the way into their season. It was a very different setup than we were used to as they played only around two games a month, which would take some getting used to for us. The team was littered with local lads and players from various parts of the world who had not made the grade in their home countries for whatever reason. Once we settled in we could see that the standard of football was good and training also was pretty much the same as at home, with long runs and small-scale matches to work on technique. The real difference was that training started at 7am due to the humidity, which was unbearable.

Hong Kong is a truly fantastic place. It's a vibrant mixture of East and West, old and new. You can drive through modern roads with six lanes of traffic edged with space-age skyscrapers either side of you then take one turning and it's like going back 100 years as you're surrounded with hot, bustling markets with snake butchers, live animals hanging up to be sold, and thousands of people all milling around the place. It really was an attack on all your senses with the colours, noise and smells of the place. It felt both dangerous and exciting and it was a long way from home for two men from south Bristol.

Chris and I had not really played that much after the Ashton Gate Eight episode but we acquitted ourselves well and it did not take long to get up to speed with the players around us. After a few initial games, Chris and I were moved from the hotel into our own two-bedroom apartment across the harbour in an area called Kowloon. I think the club started to realise how much it would cost to have us in the hotel for a long time, so the apartment was a cheaper option. The apartment was tiny with no air conditioning, which just made the place like an oven. I remember putting one of my jackets in the wardrobe slightly wet and with the humidity, by the time I came to take it out half of it had rotted away.

The only good thing about the place in Kowloon was it was right next to a park where the club trained on a weekend, so for us it was just a short walk that meant we could stay longer in our beds. The apartment also meant we could cook for ourselves sometimes instead of going to a restaurant and wondering what was going to come out of the kitchen. We were starting to settle in and we were allowed a two-minute call to home which was organised by the club's owner, Veronica. Although these calls were wonderful they really put you on a downer afterwards as all you could think about was home. Wendy, to her credit, did write to me every week but I found it hard to write back if I'm honest.

It was during one of our calls that she informed me that Bristol City had held the testimonial that was promised to the eight of us. It was Southampton v Ipswich Town at Ashton Gate and it had attracted a crowd of just over 6,000. Wendy had gone to represent me and she met with the other lads and their families. She told me that it was a difficult evening for everyone as it really was a token gesture by the club, who gave us all £1,000 each from the gate receipts to add to the money we were receiving for tearing up the contracts.

Although we were settling into life in Hong Kong we were both struggling really, especially Chris, who talked non-stop about returning home. We would spend many nights chatting about where our futures lay and invariably we would go back to reminiscing about the good times and the bad times at Ashton Gate. We knew our stay was for only a relatively short period of around four months so it was a case of just putting up with things to get by.

With our apartment being based in Kowloon, we would get a taxi to the harbourside every morning on our way to training then catch the Star Ferry across the water to Hong Kong harbour where we would then go to the ground. It was an exciting experience mixing with the locals during the 30-minute trip; we would be shoved and pushed as we stood up all the way. At times it was difficult to keep your balance with the amount of people moving as one. Then within a few weeks Chris found out that for an extra six pence we could get a seat on the ferry, which certainly helped in the mornings with our commute.

The social scene helped also with the main place being the Bull and Bear pub, which was a real haunt for expats and the odd footballer. We met many lads there who were in Hong Kong and playing for different teams. Graham Paddon, the former West Ham United and Norwich City player, had just joined Caroline Hill and he would often come out with us. Another regular was Tony Pulis, who had signed for Hong Kong Rangers. I got on really well with Tony; we had played against each other many times back in Bristol as he was ex-Rovers and we loved the banter between us. He became a really good friend out there to both me and Chris.

It was after a night in the Bull and Bear that Chris scared me half to death and even today memories of this incident leave me cold. We had been out drinking when I decided to go back to the apartment while Chris stayed in the bar. I was in bed and heard a knocking on the window. We were eight floors up so I knew it couldn't be anyone outside but the knocking persisted. In the end I managed to find the light switch in what was the darkest apartment you could imagine, and after turning the lights on I went to the curtains and opened them where I was presented with Chris, who was outside asking to be let in as I had the key. Chris had climbed eight floors up. After my initial shock I explained to him that I couldn't let him in as there were bars on our windows, so he had to climb back down so that I could open the communal door. As I shut the curtains I could hear Chinese voices shouting with Chris just going 'sorry, sorry' as he negotiated his way down the building through residents' balconies. It's a wonder he never got killed. After that, we arranged to leave a key inside a plant pot outside the building but that plan had to be abandoned when while rummaging for the key Chris discovered the pot we chose was being used as a toilet by every dog in the area. To say he wasn't pleased is an understatement.

Another crazy incident was when we were going to Repulse Bay. It was a beautiful spot with lovely clear water and white sands and we found it a welcome retreat away from the hustle and bustle of the city, as many residents of Hong Kong did. Every time I sat on the beach I would think about Wendy and the kids and how they would love it there. Me and Chris went whenever we got the chance. We used to get the local bus to the bay and the incident in question happened while waiting for one journey. We were stood on the pavement with the traffic going past when all of a sudden a women jumped from a high-rise tower block and landed with a thud in the road in front of us. We were beyond shocked. She had also slit her throat before she fell and was still holding the knife in her hand. As you can imagine there was chaos but I think the authorities were more interested in the fact that she was causing a traffic jam than anything else, but that was Hong Kong for you.

Another one of our regular visits was to a place called The DaDa, a popular place where you could eat and go shopping. We would go every weekend for breakfast and a chance to get the *South China Post* newspaper to catch up on the football back home. It wasn't easy reading for us as we missed what was happening in England, but we looked at all the results and first of all Bristol

City. They were now a new club but still struggling results-wise and although they had not treated us right, the crazy thing was that we still loved them and when they won we were happy all day. I would love to say that we laughed and joked when they lost but that was not the case. Whatever they did, they were still our club and that still continues to this day.

Me and Chris were enjoying life in Hong Kong and as we knew it was never going to be for long we just accepted the way they did things, especially within the club, even if some of their methods before and during games were a bit strange. For instance, before a match we would have to walk a pig around the centre spot and both goal areas and get it blessed to give us good luck. Maybe we should have tried that at Ashton Gate when we couldn't get a win from anywhere.

There was also the time before a big match with South China, who were also owned by Veronica, that we went to a training camp on an island in the middle of the jungle. The game was important and we were dispatched by boat to a place called Wu Kai Sha, in the north-west region of Hong Kong. It was on a remote island and we were to stay there for a few days to train before the match. I had never seen anything like it; we were speechless. We hiked through the jungle and came to a clearing with a few timber huts and a football pitch marked out on the dirt. Apparently this would be our home for a few days.

We just thought we would go with the flow but that was before we had a meal in the restaurant, and that's a term I use very loosely. The cook offered us ham and chips and we said yes enthusiastically, but there were rats and snakes scurrying around our feet as we tried to eat the food and I have never wanted Beryl and Arthur's ham and chips from the Robins Café so much in all my life. We told the lads that we couldn't eat there, and fair play to Veronica, she was told about it and then arrived at the island in a luxury cabin cruiser where she had us eat with her and some of the club's dignitaries during our stay.

It was just another example of us being a million miles away from what these people were about and we were so careful not to offend them, but some of the situations were really hard, particularly with food.

After a gruelling training camp, and I don't mean physically, we played the game against South China and were winning 1-0 until one of the young lads gave a penalty away for no reason whatsoever. I really couldn't fathom it out but nobody seemed bothered as a draw was the perfect result for both clubs. Not even Chris seemed fussed; maybe I was naive but Chris would say many times that with clubs owned by betting syndicates and some people owning two or three it was all, as he put it, 'bent'. I remember looking back at some of the games we played in and thinking maybe he was right. It certainly left a bitter taste in the mouth.

After that result, we were told our next match would be just over a month away and the club had already secured the services of Mike Channon, Steve Williams and David Armstrong from the UK to bolster the side. The thought of waiting for another month to play a competitive game mixed with the thought that maybe the result would be what both the owners wanted or decisions would be shrouded in suspicion made us realise that we were ready to come home, so we arranged a meeting with Veronica to tell her our plans. She was far from happy but we were adamant that this was it; our stay was certainly eventful but now it was time to think about our families and return home.

We had played around six games and had been away from home for three months. The result of us leaving 'early' as the club put it was that we did not get our final pay, which was really disappointing, and we also had to pay our own fare home. What added to the disappointment was that Bristol City had stopped the final payment of our redundancy because we had gone to Hong Kong. Our move was deemed as mitigating earnings, which meant for instance if you received six months' redundancy pay from an employer and you got a job after five months they could withhold the last month of pay. When I heard the news from Wendy I wasn't even surprised that they acted in this way; it was just indicative of the way the club had behaved. Everything seemed to get to a point where coming home was for the best so Chris and myself said goodbye to the lads and wished them well. We then set off for the airport and the flight home. We could not wait for a well-earned reunion with our families. Hong Kong had been an experience but there was nothing like being home.

13

Have Boots Will Travel

IT WAS great to be home from Hong Kong. Moving there certainly was not a disaster, but it was a real experience for both Chris and me. I took many positives from the trip; the place was unbelievable, and it was always good to see how other countries were and to experience their cultures. The only real downside for us was that we never got all the money we were owed by Caroline Hill.

I was now back home and reality started to settle in as I went back to the farm to make ends meet. While I was away there was no talk of other clubs offering me any contracts so as far as I was concerned football was finished for me and my future, albeit a rather unclear one, lay with the farm or making a living in any way I could. I found it frustrating that to a certain degree when you've played football and have been lucky with injuries, you could pretty much plan when you wanted to finish but I never had that. In reality football finished me and it was a lot sooner than I had ever hoped or imagined. I was 31 years of age and I still felt I could play at a decent level but football to a certain degree looks after you and when you're out you are on your own.

I met up with Chris a few times and the fact that we lost out on some of our money in Hong Kong still rankled with us, so we decided to speak to *Daily Mirror* journalist Tom Baker, who was a friend of Chris. We explained to Tom that maybe it would be a good story to write about our time in Hong Kong and lift the lid on the corruption regarding betting syndicates out there. Tom thought it was a great idea and there would also be a few quid in it for us, which we thought would make up for some of the money we were owed. Tom did a brief interview with us which the *Mirror* published as a taster for the main article, due to appear a few weeks later.

A few days after the article appeared I received a call from a Chinese-speaking gentleman who, in broken English, told me that should the main piece come out exposing the betting in Hong Kong then me or my family would be hurt. With that, he hung up. I immediately went cold. As a family we received many calls like that during the Ashton Gate Eight period but there was something about this that made me take it very seriously. I contacted Chris and Tom and we decided to cancel the story. We had hit a nerve with some people, whether that was in the UK or abroad, but we did not want to put ourselves or our families in any danger. We agreed that moving forward the best thing was to just put the missing Hong Kong money down to experience.

I continued working for Rex Baker on his farm but, brilliant though Rex was, the pay wasn't great. It was still work, however. After another long day I received a call when I got home from an agent called Dennis Roach, who asked me what I was up to. I told him I was more or less finished with football. Dennis then said that he and Coventry City chairman Jimmy Hill were putting together a squad of footballers to tour South Africa over a three-week-period and asked if I would be interested. I wasn't really that keen as it would mean being away from Wendy but the more he told me the more enthusiastic I became, particularly when he told me what I would be paid. He also went on to tell me the players who were already signed up: Alan Ball, Ossie Ardiles, Mario Kempes, Brian Greenhoff, Mike Channon, Ivan Golac, Dave Watson, Milija Aleksic, Stuart Pearson, Petar Borota, David Nish, Calvin Plummer and possibly Cyrille Regis and Justin Fashanu, with more to come. The team would be managed by former Wolverhampton Wanderers manager John Barnwell and would be playing six games, with two in the 60,000-capacity Ellis Park Stadium in Johannesburg and others in the township of Soweto. If I was interested I had to be at the hotel in Heathrow the very next day and we would fly out a few days later.

I came off the phone and spoke to Wendy. The way we looked at it was that football was one of the few things I could do, and if I was offered the chance to go and earn money from it then I had to do it for the sake of the family. The other side of the coin was this was a tour to South Africa, which still had an apartheid regime in place where blacks and whites were segregated. The world had imposed sanctions on South Africa due to its stance with apartheid and in particular when there were 'rebel' cricket or rugby tours, there was always a high number of demonstrations over them due to the thought that the tour in some way condoned the regime by the very fact that the teams had come to the country to play. I never really took a lot of it in because as far as I was concerned politics and sport did not mix, plus I was being paid to play football as that was what I did.

Maybe I was naive but I phoned Rex to tell him I would need a few weeks off and then called Dennis to tell him I was in. I packed hurriedly and said my goodbyes to Wendy and the kids; at least this goodbye wasn't as emotional as when I left for Hong Kong as this was very much like many of the tours I had done with Bristol City where they all lasted around two weeks tops. I made my way to the hotel just outside Heathrow and met up with some of the players, many of whom I had played against during my career and a few I had never met before. The idea was to take a party of 18 players but due to the fact that the tour was going to be in South Africa, and they were not members of FIFA, there was enormous pressure on the football authorities to stop it. With this in mind we never really knew who was definitely coming until they actually walked into the hotel.

The following day, Jimmy Hill, John Barnwell and Dennis Roach gave a press conference as news of the tour broke in the media. More pressure was then placed on the organisers to scrap it but as John said at the time, he was an out-of-work manager who had been offered a job and many of the players did not have clubs so they were just earning a living. John also said that he found apartheid abhorrent but the team were going to play against black teams in what was at the time essentially a black man's sport in South Africa. History had shown that the rich white section of the population preferred rugby as their chosen sport. As far as I was concerned he pretty much said what we as players were thinking.

We flew out to Schiphol Airport in Amsterdam to get our connecting flight to Cape Town. Unfortunately Mario Kempes, Ossie Ardiles, Alan Ball, Ivan Golac, Cyrille Regis and Justin Fashanu all had second thoughts about the trip and never came. Dennis did, however, manage to attract Billy Jennings, once of West Ham United, former Scotland and QPR midfielder Don Masson, and Frank Carrodus, who had been at Aston Villa.

Arriving in Cape Town was truly fantastic. I loved the scenery, the hills and the waves of the sea crashing into some of the most beautiful beaches I had ever seen. It really was a breathtaking country. The countryside was ever-changing; you could see the scorched red earth and then go a few miles and see rich green valleys. I was mesmerised by it all. I roomed with former Leicester City, Derby County and England full-back David Nish, who had just retired after playing in the USA for a few years and like me he thought the tour was a great opportunity to see another part of the world while earning a few quid in the process.

For the first few days we were taken to Sun City to enjoy ourselves before the tour started in earnest. Sun City was a luxury resort and casino situated in the north-west province of South

Africa, a couple of hours by plane away from Cape Town. It opened in 1979 and it was used as a place to try and attract the world's top entertainment stars to play as there was a cultural boycott of the country. It was the height of luxury and it was an incredible place for us to stay. We were even given a few quid to play the tables by the organisers of the tour. When we returned to Cape Town there was opposition and demonstrations the moment we landed but we just went straight to our hotel and planned for our first game, in the city against a Cape select XI. It ended 0-0 but there were huge demonstrations with the police fighting back the protesters outside the ground. In the stadium the crowd was around 5,000 and although there was trouble outside the fans inside loved the match and showed their appreciation to us by giving us a standing ovation at the end.

We then made the two-hour flight to Johannesburg for our next match, in the township of Soweto. It was a fascinating place covering around 40 square miles which housed over one million people who were predominantly black. The poverty was terrible with large families living in what back home would be garden sheds. It was a real shock to the system but the people were wonderful and we spent a few days putting on coaching sessions with the local children and youths. They were really responsive to us, which made for a great atmosphere away from the tension and demonstrations of the organised matches.

You really got to see a different side of South Africa away from the big cities and it was certainly a real eye-opener for all of us. The kids had no shoes or equipment but they were so skilful. The coaching sessions were a real hit with the township but the tension built days before our second game against a team called Orlando Pirates. The local TV news was full of stories about how the 'rebel' tourists were not welcome, and that was probably true, but you would not have thought that if you had seen the young kids at our sessions. I will never forget the joy on their faces while being coached by us.

Unfortunately for the organisers, Orlando Pirates pulled out of the match because of a backlash from anti-apartheid protesters, so we played a team called AmaZulu instead. The build-up to this was like a war zone with demonstrators everywhere fighting with the police who were firing tear gas and whipping the protesters with their truncheons. I later found out that the demonstration was featured on the TV back home in the UK and Wendy was watching it all unfold, much to her horror. When the game got going there were around 10,000 fans in the stadium to watch our 1-0 win. Again it was a decent match with both teams giving their all but there was now a real groundswell to get the tour stopped.

Our final fixture was in Johannesburg and we were put up at a lovely hotel right next to the stadium, so it really was a case of luxury all the way for us. We had a few days before the game so we would spend our time lying by the pool, which was on top of the hotel and had a wonderful view of the city. We mingled with the guests, including two who were very popular – TV comedienne Marti Caine and the singer and actress Olivia Newton-John. Both women were very attractive and very popular with the lads, and most of the male hotel guests. My one claim to fame is that Olivia asked me if I would like to go for a drink with her; as you can imagine I was incredibly flattered and it's a story that I always remind Wendy of to this day. I did go but I also made sure all the lads came too, so we ended up in a nightclub dancing away and having a great time. She was a lovely lady with a fantastic personality and I really used to wind the rest of the lads up that she wanted a piece of this Bedminster lad, even though some of them were giving their best lines to Olivia and Marti, but joking aside there has only ever been one woman for me – Wendy. It's a great story that I always tell, particularly when her hit film *Grease* comes on the TV.

After our rest days it was back to football and we managed a 1-1 draw with a Transvaal invitation side, with Billy Jennings getting our goal. After the game we were told that all the other teams we were due to play had pulled out of playing us. The money for the tour was put up by South Africa Breweries and there had been a boycott on their products, so along with the political pressure and violence that had shrouded the trip it was decided that it was to end after ten days. We were all disappointed that it was finishing as we had enjoyed being there, and it certainly was for me a real eye-opener to a beautiful part of the world that I would probably never see again. It also gave me a better understanding of the regime there and of how life was for certain people.

It was good to be home and I used to love telling Wendy and the kids about South Africa and what it had been like, especially when the kids would ask if I saw elephants and lions out there. When the kids were not around Wendy told me that there had been abusive calls to the home from people who thought what I was doing was disgusting. I felt terrible that she had to deal with that on her own, but I still believe what we were doing was a good thing. I felt that tour had done me good both financially and emotionally; I was pleased that I had played a decent level and held my own with some great players.

A few weeks after coming back I was approached by an old school-mate from Southville, Ivor Pope. Ivor was a good bloke who I had not seen for years and he told me that he was organising a football tournament in Ashton Park, which was not too far from where I had grown up, and he asked if I would like to play in it. I agreed, so Ivor gave me the details and that was it. A few days before the tournament he contacted me and asked if I had ever gone to South Africa. I told him I had just returned and he said, 'Oh, well there's a problem. Bristol City Council who own Ashton Park have told me that you are on a United Nations blacklist for playing football in South Africa and if you play in the tournament they will cancel it.' I did not know what to say and was astonished. I knew there might be some sort of backlash when I returned but I didn't believe it would be anything like this. I told Ivor I certainly did not want to cause him any problems so I did not go.

The problem with the blacklist came at the same time that former Bristol Rovers player Bobby Jones contacted me and asked me if I would like to come and sign for Bath City, where he was the manager. I told Bobby that there was a problem with the blacklist and he said he would look into it. Bobby really started to sell me the club and was keen for me to sign but I had my reservations; apart from this blacklist thing I was working really long hours for Rex Baker at the farm as well as doing more building and maintenance which I wanted to expand in the future if possible. Bath were part-time but I was still worried about being able to fit it all in. In the end I did not want to let him down and I agreed to sign.

Bath have a rich history in non-league football and at the time they were in the Alliance Premier League. This was in 1983 and the club had some good players such as Dave Mogg, Tony Ricketts, Shaun Penny and my old Ashton Gate Eight mate Peter Aitken, who had arrived at Bath after a spell at York City. At first I could only train due to the ban but after a few months it was lifted for all the players who took part in the tour so we were all able to play again.

I enjoyed my time at Bath but if I'm honest things were not right; deep down I think I knew I just couldn't manage everything off the field. I was working long hours, sometimes starting at five in the morning and not finishing until after ten at night with farm work, and I just did not seem to be able to fit it all in. Everything came to a head before a home game. I had been up really early seeing to the cows and I had to be at Bath's Twerton Park ground at 2pm for a 3pm kick-off. After sorting out things on the farm I went home ready for the game and sat down in the chair about midday. The next thing I knew, I woke up and saw on the clock that it was now gone 3pm. I jumped up in a panic, scrambled some gear together and got in the car and headed for Bath, arriving just after half-time. Bobby was not too pleased and he read me the riot act, saying I was unprofessional, which I admit it was. I apologised and we agreed there and then that this was not going to work out. Bobby was a great bloke and the club was also a good place to be, but it was the right thing for me to finish even though I had only played 12 games for them.

Looking back at this period of time I went from club to club but never really covered myself in glory as it was as though I never wanted to let anyone down, but in truth I just wasn't thinking straight. After Bath I was still in demand and I played one game at Yeovil Town, eight times for Gloucester City, I made a few appearances for Forest Green Rovers and then signed for Western League Minehead Town in 1985 aged 34. All these clubs were great and the lads everywhere welcomed me in with no problems but I just felt I let them and myself down by not really being able to commit due to the financial and work pressures I had outside the game, combined with my head not being in the right place.

It was while I was at Minehead that the Bristol football community was shocked by the death of Bristol Rovers' highly rated winger Mike Barrett due to cancer at the age of 23. Mike was a real star for Rovers and he had a massive future ahead of him. His death was tragic as he left a wife and children. I had known him briefly but I had some good friends who were ex-Rovers and Mike's funeral was a way for the two Bristol clubs to come together to pay their respects to him. I attended the gathering and although it was a very sad affair it was good to catch up with a few old City team-mates and some Rovers friends who I used to kick lumps out of when we played against each other. After the service I was chatting outside the church when the Rovers manager Dave Williams approached me and asked what I was up to. Dave had been in the job for a few seasons having played for them as well as Norwich City. I told him that I was at Minehead and it was good except for the 120-mile round trip, which was difficult in midweek and especially with work. I also explained that I missed the banter and training that went with being a professional footballer.

Dave understood what I was saying then then out of the blue he asked if I would consider signing for Rovers as a non-contract player and playing in the reserves. He pointed out that with my experience I would be an asset to the youngsters in the team. I was flattered and said that I would have to get in real shape for reserve team football but I would think about it. On the drive home I mulled it over and over and that evening I talked it through with Wendy. I don't know what it was about the opportunity that appealed to me so much; no disrespect to the other sides I had played for but maybe it was being back in a league club setup and having the chance to pass on some knowledge to youngsters coming through that lit some sort of spark in me. I realised that for this to happen I would have to speak to Minehead and sort something out with Rex at the farm. This I did and Minehead were great, while Rex allowed me to have a few mornings off for training plus any time off for games. I was also being paid at Rovers, not a lot, but the whole thing meant so much to me.

I arrived at Rovers' training ground at Hambrook on the outskirts of Bristol and the banter started immediately within the first team players and the backroom staff, ribbing me about my City days. Rovers were in the Third Division and the first team had some really good players such as Paul Randall, Ian Holloway and Steve White, as well as my old Bristol City team-mate Ray Cashley. Looking after the youth team was Harold Jarman, while Wayne Jones was Dave's assistant. They had both played for Rovers. I loved it from the moment I arrived. They were brilliant towards me and I will never forget it.

The reserves played in the Combination League and I played with some great lads who always wanted to learn, and although we sometimes got beaten heavily it wasn't necessarily about the result – it was about the youngsters learning. I went all over the country playing again in some of the great grounds I had played in during my time with Bristol City, such as Stamford Bridge, Highbury and White Hart Lane, and in front of some decent crowds. I was even in contention for the first team at one point when Rovers were drawn against Arsenal at Highbury in the League Cup. Due to injuries there were whispers that I might get a game even though I was now 34 years old. I laughed them off but inside I was starting to get a bit excited, although it never happened in the end.

My whole time at Bristol Rovers was incredible. There I was, a staunch City fan and player who had played many times against their big rivals, but Rovers' supporters were great with me as were all the staff and players. Although I was only there for a season, it is a time I will never forget. It seemed to sort me out and put me in the right direction as far as playing again; it was like it was my proper farewell to the game. After having that season I was now ready to almost put football to bed and take on the rest of my life and carve a proper business that would sustain me and the family for the long term.

14

Tough Times

LEAVING BRISTOL Rovers after one season really was a double-edged sword. I was gutted that it came to an end but turning out for them for that season really seemed to put my football career to a logical end. It was also an end that was easier to take in terms of how I wanted to finish playing. I had done well at Rovers and made some great friends but I realised that playing at great grounds again, even though they were not packed to the rafters, was enough for me to say goodbye to the game, certainly at that level. In some ways it brought back my love of football.

Chris Garland said the same when he re-joined Bristol City while they were in the Fourth Division. Chris had felt damaged by the Ashton Gate Eight affair but the fact that he had the chance to pull on that shirt again healed the pain he felt about leaving City. I unfortunately never got the chance to do what Chris did but playing in the blue and white quarters of Rovers helped me in the same way.

Away from football, I was starting to get more and more work in the building industry. I left the farm to concentrate solely on trying to develop some sort of business, which I did. We were now living in Nailsea and although I certainly wasn't rolling in cash it was providing a living for me and the family. My first employee was a lovely guy called Dane Leman, who was really keen and he just learned his building skills on the job. We would never say no to work no matter how dirty or terrible it was; as far as I was concerned it was work and it was not to be turned down in any shape or form. I recall how people used to look at me and be amazed to see me knocking down walls or spending a day on a jack hammer. You could see them thinking, 'Is that Geoff Merrick?' I'm sure they must have thought I was a millionaire and did not know why I was up to my eyes in dust and dirt. They would love to talk about football and Bristol City and I was happy to sit and chat with them.

It was odd looking back though; I worked like a trojan and I remember my brother saying to me, 'What are you trying to prove, Geoff?' and I think I was trying to prove that I did not need football and I could be just as successful without it. The truth was I still missed football even though I would tell customers and friends that I didn't miss it at all. Business boomed as we took on more and more projects and employees. But the call of football was never that far away, although it came with a different atmosphere. I became friends with a plasterer called Peter McColl. Pete was a smashing bloke and he was the manager of local Somerset County League side Shirehampton FC. He begged me to turn out for them and in the end he made me an offer I couldn't refuse. I was struggling to get plasterers for jobs so he said that if I came to play for them he would teach me to plaster. Happy days, I thought so that's what we did, although I wasn't the greatest pupil.

Playing at Shirehampton was fantastic. They were a great bunch of lads, many of whom were in the building trade, so we had a common interest. I would work Monday to Friday and really enjoy going for a match on a Saturday and maybe a pint afterwards. Pete had created a great team spirit among the lads and they all took the piss and welcomed me with open arms, which was great. The football was of a good standard but I played with an air of freedom which I had never really had before. The pressures of professional football were certainly not there now. The majority of the opposition were great and always wanted to chat about my career, but there were a few who tried to make a name for themselves by kicking a former player up in the air. I recall getting a few broken ribs in one match courtesy of an opposing keeper who decided to flex his muscles. It didn't bother me ego-wise but my first thought when I got an injury was always that I hoped I would be okay for work on the Monday.

I have great affection for the lads at Shirehampton and I only hope my performances on the pitch for them were better than my plastering skills. Thinking about it, Pete certainly got the better side of the deal. I was there for a few years before switching to Nailsea Town which again was a fantastic atmosphere. Nailsea were also in the Somerset County League and this time I had the added bonus of being able to play with my two sons, Elliott and

Luke, which was such a thrill for me. The football was a good standard and the lads were all great.

My building work was certainly booming with all the family involved in the business, but things started to expand at a massive rate and this wasn't always appreciated by our neighbours. Our house in Nailsea was in a lovely road but at times we would have six or seven work vans parked along the road, which wasn't great, and in the end one of the neighbours complained to the council so we had to look for new premises. We found a farm on the outskirts of Nailsea with around five acres of land, so it was perfect. I knew the previous owners and jumped at the chance to own it. The farm has always been a bit of a sanctuary for me throughout my life and although I wasn't farming as such when we moved in, there is something about being in the countryside that I have always felt at peace with right from the age of 11 when I went to work out at Long Ashton for a few pennies. And whenever life has thrown me some sort of curve ball, which it has done plenty of times, it's the farm where I have gone to take stock of things and come back fighting.

The place was a godsend for us in terms of storage and building materials as we grew and grew and at one point I had 46 men working for me at a job in Weymouth plus a further ten on a hotel in Hereford. I loved the work, and building sites, although tough places to work, were incredibly similar to a football dressing room with piss-taking, wind-ups and all sorts of banter going on. I recall on one site when all of the lads ripped the piss out of me due to one of my own goals for Bristol City being shown on the TV that weekend. They were relentless but I loved it if I'm honest; we were a real band of brothers.

The ferocity of the work, though, really did put an end to my footballing career once and for all. There had been a few occasions at Nailsea Town where myself, Luke and Elliott – who were working with me – had raced from a site to make kick-off just by the skin of our teeth. But once we were coming back from Hereford where we had been on a job and we nearly never made it due to traffic and workload, and it was then I decided that this couldn't go on so to be fair to my old farm buddy Rex Baker – who was running the club at the time – and the lads in the team I decided to hang up the Merrick boots forever. I was 46 years of age and it really was time to finish up; my body was really feeling it yet the last few years of my playing days had been some of the best times in the whole of my career so there were no regrets about giving up. Things had come to a natural end and it was time to move on.

The building trade can be a harsh and unforgiving place. We had worked hard to get a reputation as a family-run company that gave excellent service. It was interesting that being Geoff Merrick plainly and rightly made no difference in terms of reputation in the trade, so although clients knew me through my days in football I had to make a new name for myself in the building industry through reliability and good work. As a company we rolled with the punches at times, particularly through the recession of the early 1990s, when things were difficult but we managed to keep going for our staff. That's how the building game is; it's either feast or famine. It can be a brutal industry to try and earn a living in.

A few years after seeing ourselves through a tough time we were hit by a second recession which completely floored us. Companies we had completed work for never paid up what was owed and then there would be times when they went back on agreed deals with us. We were getting into more and more trouble with cashflow. I had invested heavily in the business but we were being welshed on by people who owed us money; there were certainly no morals or integrity shown by large companies in the trade at that time. I was owed money left, right and centre. It would be £40,000 here then £30,000 there, then the banks wanted their money back to recoup their losses and it sent me into insolvency so I re-mortgaged the farm so I would have money to pay the bank back what I owed while also paying anybody who I owed money to. It was a dreadful time for all of us, not only in the family but those in the company too. It broke my heart to have to re-mortgage as I knew the farm, even today, would never be my own but it was the right thing to do. Life again had sent us another test, but as the head of the family I knew I would have to navigate our way out of it, as I have always done.

That period in my life leaves me cold when I think about it today. We lost some great people and the strength all my family showed during that time, not only as individuals but as a support to me, will stay with me forever. After the whole dreadful affair it was a case of finding sanctuary again in the farm as the kids started to leave home and carve out their own lives, so Wendy and I decided that we would throw ourselves fully into farming life. I was still doing little building jobs but nothing on the scale that I had been. We decided to buy six Belgian Blue Heifer cows and keep them on the farm. They were like children for me. I would bucket feed them around five in the morning until late into the night. I remember my long-standing friend Rex Baker telling us that they were ready for slaughter but we just looked at him and said, 'Well that won't be happening,' so we decided to breed them. They gave us such joy even though they were hard work. We delivered calves and we got enormous pleasure from that.

I ended up renting a further 30 acres from my neighbour and friend Colin Pike and as we stand today I have 52 cows with four of them being from the original six Belgian Blue Heifers. My life on the farm, although extremely tough in terms of work, is priceless. As I have said many times, it's where me, Wendy and our Dalmatian Bert are at peace. We have some fantastic people around us who are always there with help and to give advice when needed, and it's idyllic, although a few years ago things could have taken a very different road for me and the family.

It was a Sunday and we were having some relatives round for a meal and a drink. I was rushing around here and there getting things ready outside on the farm so I would be free for our guests.

I didn't feel too well and I was having a lot of acid in my chest, which was causing me discomfort, while my head was just feeling a bit fuzzy. I was relatively okay but at one point I nearly keeled over, although I just managed to stop myself and stay upright. I never mentioned it to Wendy, we had a lovely afternoon with our relatives, and I thought nothing of it. On the Monday I felt the same but just got on with things. Tuesday arrived and Wendy had to go to the doctor for an appointment. I drove her and while Wendy was being seen to, the doctor said to me, 'Are you okay, Geoff? You look terrible.' I told her how I had been feeling and she took my blood pressure and told me that she was calling for an ambulance as in her opinion I'd had a heart attack and she was sending me to the Bristol Royal Infirmary immediately. I didn't really know what to say.

The ambulance turned up and the paramedics put me at ease by telling me they thought I had not had a heart attack, but they were taking me in anyway. When I got to the hospital I was put on a bed and checked over by a nurse who again assured me I had not had a heart attack, but a few minutes later she came back in and said they had looked at my tests and I had indeed had one. I was amazed. I know I felt rough but I imagined a heart attack was like you see in the films where people grab their chests gasping for breath, and it had been nothing like that. They told me I would be moved to a ward and would be in hospital for a while as they were going to fit me with a stent. My immediate thoughts were about my cows as they needed feeding. I phoned Charlie and she asked Rex Baker and Rich Dyer, my two old pals, if they would help out, which they duly did.

I was in hospital for a week and when I left they told me that I should rest up for at least three weeks. I did so for two then went back to working on the farm along with Rex and Rich, but I certainly felt that I had been hit by a steam hammer. I struggled with most tasks and I don't think I have ever really been the same since in terms of fitness. I can't thank Rex and Rich enough for helping me out during that time. That's the thing with farming, it doesn't stop so you can have a day off, animals need your care and attention all the time. It wasn't as if I could have sat in the chair for a few weeks. Things had to be done. Again it was another drama that was thrown at me but I managed to work my way around it, even if the consequences were bigger than anything I had faced before. When I went back to the consultant she told me she couldn't believe how well I had recovered as when she saw me I was very, very ill as she put it.

I often walk the fields with Bert and think about the various things that have happened to me in my life. There is a piece of me that is proud that whatever gets thrown at me I have managed to navigate my way out of it and survive. I suppose I have always had a survival instinct but never knew it until later in my life. Wendy and the kids have always meant the world to me, as do my eight grandchildren, and as far as family are concerned I'm a millionaire as what they give me is something that you could not buy. That love and support is something that I have had all my life with the people who have been close to me or guided me in the right direction. Whether it was my mum and dad, my brother Vernon, school teachers and close friends, I have always felt loved and supported by them all. Feeling like that is truly priceless.

15
Family

FAMILY, AS you may have guessed, has always been incredibly important to me and I suppose it's the same for any sportsperson. They have to follow a career in the public eye while also protect their family from all the things that come with it. Neil wanted to hand this chapter over to my children and Wendy for their take on living with me.

It's a chapter that I won't see until this book is released, so I hope they have been kind about me.

Charlie

As the oldest, I do remember a time before two very annoying twins arrived in the Merrick household. When Mum was in hospital having Luke and Elliott, Dad was racing from professional footballer to doting father, which to his credit he did admirably as Mum had to stay in for a while due to complications with the birth and the boys. He would take me to the ground at times and even in the dressing room where I would just shut my eyes as all the City lads got dressed. I'm sure it's not the sort of thing that would be done today but I do look back on it with a certain amount of amazement.

When Dad was playing my usual place to stay was with Auntie May, who lived with my grandparents on Garnett Street in Bedminster. I loved it there as they would all dote on me. As I got older I started to realise that Dad was famous around the city. I was always aware that he played for Bristol City but going to games and seeing him in the paper just seemed the norm.

I had a great life as a kid. We were not spoilt but always had nice things and particularly at Christmas when we always got what we wanted, but Dad always instilled the value of things – not in a monetary sense but always telling us that there were people who did not have the life we did. He taught us the value of working hard to get stuff as we got older, which is something I have always instilled in my own children.

There was a real community among all the children of the Bristol City team. We met up at games and played together, and the Christmas parties the club put on for us were brilliant. I remember Luke and Elliott sat on Father Christmas's knee and both were trying to pull his beard off, but it showed how good the parties were as it was his own white beard. I'm sure the poor chap was in agony.

I do remember the whole Ashton Gate Eight saga and although I did not understand everything that went on, Dad did inform us that our circumstances in terms of finance were about to change.

I also have a recollection of watching an old video of his Bristol City games at home with him. I was only young and it was just after he left the club and there was a certain game on, probably the promotion game against Portsmouth and I looked back and he was crying. Dad wasn't an emotional man and I will never forget it as the fact that he was so upset made me cry as well.

Things did change for us, although he fought tooth and nail to keep our house, which was in jeopardy many times. It really kicked in when he went away to places like Hong Kong or South Africa. This wasn't like the times he went away with the club, when you could play with the other players' kids and Mum could chat to the other wives. This was something else and I really missed him. I remember having a map on the wall in my bedroom with Hong Kong marked on it and one day I just ripped it off in frustration that he wasn't with us. I wanted him home. I do now realise why he went away and to a certain extent I'm really proud of him in the way that he did what he could to keep a roof over our heads and food on the table.

Dad has always been a survivor and I really admire that about him. He has always given us the best advice. When I was at school I loved sport and he would be encouraging but not in a pushy parent way, but equally when things like drama popped up for me to do, which was a subject I hated, he would tell me to do it and face things I was afraid of. Never run from a difficult task.

This was the same when I bought a horse box for my horse and I was nervous to take it out on the roads. What did he do? He took me out and he made sure I went around the most difficult hills and junctions all around the Nailsea and Backwell area, knowing that once I had done it I would be okay. He was the same when I worked for him in the building business. He would give me difficult tasks in the office knowing I could complete them even if at first I didn't think I could.

I am incredibly proud of him and what he has achieved in his life. Dad is a brilliant grandfather who lets the kids make mistakes and tells them to learn from them. He and Mum taught all of us proper values and respect, which we have hopefully passed on to our own children. I love it when people know whose daughter I am and they want to talk about him. This happens everywhere, even abroad; when they find out and talk about Dad there is real affection for him which is lovely. He is my father and whatever life throws at him he has always been able to steer a course to safety for him, Mum and the family. He is a very special man.

Luke

I suppose I was always aware of what Dad did for a living as Bristol City Football Club was such a massive part of family life growing up. I recall Dad picking me up from primary school and school-mates flocking to the car window to see him and get an autograph. It was the same when as children we got taken to matches at Ashton Gate and he would be constantly stopped by fans who wanted to talk to him or get a signature.

Me and Elliott were too young really to understand the Ashton Gate Eight drama but we knew that things were not the same for us. I remember the TV cameras were everywhere around our street and we were in the paper and on the TV a lot but I never really knew why.

I have a vivid memory of when Dad left Bristol City and went with Chris Garland to Hong Kong. We were just told that he had gone away with football but he would be away a bit longer than usual. We all really missed him and I recall he left his car, a VW Passat, on the drive. Mum did not drive so she lent it to Trish, Chris's wife, and I distinctly remember me and Charlie out on our bikes and seeing the car heading for home. We were thrilled as we thought it was Dad, so we pedalled like mad to catch up with it but when we got home it was just Trish visiting Mum. Me and Charlie were really upset. When Dad was in Hong Kong he would phone Mum every week and I know she would be upset after the call as they missed each other so much. I think that's why we rarely spoke to him down the phone as Mum knew it would upset him.

When I look back at times like that I am incredibly proud of him for the way he did his best for his family, and always has done for us. He was a wonderful father when we were all younger and I know it was difficult for him as he was always busy with football, and at times the family suffered due to him having to go away, but even from an early age I knew he would always be there for me. As I have got older I feel I have understood him more due to the fact that I now understand some of the things that he has been through.

I remember when me and Elliott were about 15 we were good footballers and would play with him in various ex-City and celebrity games. After one match, the Bristol City youth boss, Dad's old team-mate Gerry Sweeney, asked us to come and play with the youth team on a regular basis. Dad was cool to the idea and he certainly never pushed us into trying to make it a career. Looking back he did not want us to enter a game that would at times treat people with such a lack of respect. I think that's why he never wanted to take up coaching or management even though he would have been a natural at it.

As we got older Elliott and myself got to play with him at Nailsea Town and it was a fantastic time of our lives. We had some great players including Ryan Garland, the son of Chris, and there were also ex-City players Howard Pritchard and Ricky Chandler. Dad loved those times and it was great to see him enjoying his football again. We were now also working with him in his building company and again he was so driven in what he wanted to achieve that I was in awe of him.

He is a loving father but he is also hard; he taught us all from an early age the value of things and how you had to work for them. He also has taught us not to be soft and to make sure, particularly in our careers, that we were not pushed around. I have always thought Dad has had an incredible life and he is a real inspiration to not only his family but to other people. He has had some blows but he survived them and nothing will knock him down.

I see what he means to people, particularly City fans. When we have been invited to functions at the club they speak to him with such affection that it makes me really proud that he's my dad. I remember once there was an event for Chris Garland's testimonial, which I attended with Dad. There was a Q&A session where people were asking about the Ashton Gate Eight and Dad was getting asked about what really happened. Some people on the table were trying to get him to not say anything but I was telling him, 'Tell them the truth, Dad.' In the end he did and afterwards there were people coming up to him in tears over the way he was treated, saying they never truly knew the facts.

I have always been pushing him to tell his story as I want people to know not only the facts of the Ashton Gate Eight affair but what a fantastic life he has led. I also think doing the book with Neil has helped him come to terms with some of the things that have happened to him. I think it's been a really healthy exercise for him talking about the old days and how he feels now towards those events. He is certainly better for the experience.

There is not a lot more I can say about him – only that he is an incredibly special husband, father and grandfather and he means the world to all of us.

Elliott

My early memories are of everybody wanting to talk to Dad. I found it all a bit weird, especially when I was a pupil at Golden Valley Primary School in Nailsea and my teacher would say, 'Oh

I saw your dad on telly last night.' I missed the big part of Dad's career but I remember all the TV crews up and down the street where we lived in Nailsea filming us as a family during the Ashton Gate Eight saga. It was a time that Dad never really spoke about until years later when we were grown up, although I do remember him explaining that things may be a bit different for us.

Even when it all died down he would still take me and Luke to Ashton Gate to see a game but he would queue up and pay and we would stand on the terraces with him. Fans were brilliant with him, always asking for an autograph and asking how he was and what he was doing. I used to be really proud of how much they loved him.

We are a close-knit family and that means everything to Mum and Dad. He has never been the sort of dad who is overbearing, in fact he is very much in the background, but you know whatever you do he is always there for you to give advice. I remember when Luke and I left our jobs to join the family building firm, he started us at the bottom as labourers and we gradually worked our way up to running things with Dad. He made sure you had no quick route to the top because as far as he was concerned you had to prove you were worth it, and it certainly made us better for it. We had some great times on the building sites with him and the company went from strength to strength, turning over around a million and a half of business at one point, but the recession killed it. It was a difficult time for everybody, especially us as a family, but he dusted himself down and had the strength of character to carry on with the farm, which makes me incredibly proud.

We also shared some great times with Nailsea Town. You could still see that Dad had all the skills and read the game like nobody I had ever seen. We had a great team with players like Dad, Dave Payne, Ricky Chandler and Howard Pritchard. Howard in particular was a big influence on the pitch for me and Luke as he was a really talented player. He was also a driving instructor and would take us for driving lessons but drive us to the Royal Oak pub in Nailsea afterwards, so I'm not sure he was as good an influence off the pitch. I talk about these times with Dad a lot and it was great to see him play football in an almost carefree fashion. You could tell he enjoyed it but the work demands on him forced him to retire from the game.

Dad is a survivor. He has had some hard times over the years but he navigates himself through them, always putting the family at the forefront of everything he does. It's also great to see how loved he is by the fans of Bristol City and the ex-players from the 1970s, and it is always an honour to be in their company along with Dad when they are talking about old times. Dad is a really modest man who never seeks the limelight and over the years we have talked more about his career and the things that happened to him. I feel I understand him more now and I am incredibly proud of the father he is to us.

Wendy

Well, what can I say about Geoff? He is the love of my life and we have been together for over 50 years. I remember when I first met him down at Burnham. I'm not saying it was love at first sight but it didn't take long for me to know he was the right one for me. I didn't know too much about football at the time but I soon got to realise that it would engulf our family, not only in a good way but also putting us through some terrible times.

I stayed in Bedminster with Geoff and his parents for a couple of years before we got married, and I remember him giving up his bed for me so he had to sleep on the settee, which even to this day he claims stunted his growth. He said if he had a proper bed he would have been six foot two in height.

Geoff's mum and dad were the most wonderful people who treated me like a daughter from the word go and the four of us had some great times together. I remember we all went to the Bierkeller which was a large German pub in the centre of Bristol. Geoff's dad didn't drink that much but on this night we were having such a great time that he certainly overdid things. As Geoff drove us home his dad was singing rugby songs in the passenger seat and telling me dirty jokes. Geoff couldn't believe it, saying that he had never told him any dirty jokes, and that I had corrupted his dad. It was so funny but it showed how relaxed we all were with each other. They were a very special couple who instilled values and honesty in Geoff.

I have always been immensely proud of him and when he was captain of City he always went to different functions and made all sorts of speeches, even though he is very much a man who is happy in the background like his dad was. We both look upon those days with such affection as the whole of the club were like an extended family for everyone as we all knew each other and each other's children. He loved the club, although he was terrible to live with when City lost as he would dissect every minute of the game to see if he could have done better and always seemed to blame himself when they lost and praised other people when the won. That's just how he is.

We have been through so much together and I remember that terrible day in 1982 when he came home and told me he had been sacked and had no job. I really couldn't believe that something like that could happen but we got through things together as a family and when he went away to places like Hong Kong I was so worried about him but I knew he was prepared to do anything for us to keep a roof over our heads.

Life has not been easy and when he had his heart attack a few years ago I was worried to death for him but in true Geoff Merrick style he got through, although I think the whole event hit him quite hard as he has always thought he was indestructible. He still manages to work hard on the farm and with the animals he loves so much. He has a heart of gold and he would do anything for his family and I love him with all my heart.

16
Reflections

SO THIS is it, the last chapter of the book. I hope you have got something out of it in terms of maybe understanding a bit more about not only Geoff the footballer but Geoff the man. On a personal note I have found the whole process of writing this very cathartic. I have tried to be honest and respectful towards people who have been involved in every aspect of my life while also being true to myself, and I hope that comes across. I have also been able to reflect on both my football career and my life outside the game.

During the writing process I unearthed and dissected different feelings I had during my life, and looking at the book laid out in front of me today it's easy to see now that there were certainly bouts of depression that went with the injuries, the Ashton Gate Eight saga and the difficult times with my own building company that I have never previously addressed, not to mention my health scare, until I confronted them in this book. I come from a different era where personal feelings and things are not really spoken about. It's very much a case of getting on with things so to be able to get these stories off my chest and down on paper has been immensely helpful to me.

Working with Neil has been a real joy and I will certainly miss our regular Wednesday get-togethers. I have laughed and cried at certain points in the book and it's strange how certain memories have triggered others to come to the surface and end up on the pages. I said at the start of this journey that I wanted to do a book and put many things to bed, which is why I said to Neil at the very start that I was going to tell my story then that would be it, no more talking about the Ashton Gate Eight, so I hope my story will do this.

Much has been written about me over the years and many assumptions have been made, particularly when it comes to the Ashton Gate Eight and Bristol City in general. Despite that terrible time in my life my love for the club will never fade. City have always been at my very heart from the moment I walked through the entrance all those years ago. The people who were there were very special and any success we achieved was down to not only the players on the pitch but everybody, from chairman to programme seller. We were a big family. Take Harry and Marina Dolman, who looked after me and were a very special couple. Harry encouraged me and Marina is still a trusted friend even today.

Then you have Fred Ford, who was different class. Fred was rugged and straight out of the 1950s, and my relationship with him was one of admiration and fear – if he was coming down a corridor towards you then you would hide as he would probably want to know what you were doing. I never played first team football for Fred but I knew he believed in me. I recall all us apprentices in a circle with Fred in the middle reading us the riot act as he thought we should bc training more. He went round each of us saying, 'You won't make it, you won't make it, you won't make it,' and then he got to me and said, 'You will have to work harder.' I never forgot that and it made me feel at the time that maybe Fred thought I had a chance. As my career progressed I realised how special he was and we would meet up and chat about how I was doing. In the end I was honoured to call him my friend.

Another manager I have to speak about is Alan Dicks. To the outside world I suppose people thought I was his right-hand man but that wasn't really the case. I had huge respect for Alan and I admired him. When he first arrived at the club it was difficult for him as many of the players were not that enthusiastic about his new methods. I suppose he could not have been a bigger contrast to Fred. But he persevered and made difficult decisions to remove many loved players and bring in his own group, which in the end became Bristol City's most successful team to date. On a personal note I know I was his captain but we used to clash occasionally, particularly if the lads were unhappy about something and I would always speak to Alan on their behalf. To his credit he was always professional and he created a dressing room where opinions were encouraged. Alan was always fair but I never got the feeling from him that he thought I was one of his better players. He never looked upon me the same way he looked upon, say, Gerry Gow. There weren't many pats on the back or words of encouragement. But to give Alan the benefit of the doubt, he would probably say he never needed to with me.

All that aside, we shared a wonderful journey together along with every one of the promotion squad: Cashley, Sweeney, Drysdale, Brolly, Cheesley, Collier, Emanuel, Fear, Gillies, Gow, Mann, Ritchie, Sweeney, Tainton, Whitehead, Harding, McNeill. We used 17 players that promotion year and 11 came through the youth team, which was incredible. Just reeling off those names today sparks so many memories in me that I get quite emotional thinking about them. They were all my friends and we were such a great group together. Training used to be such an enjoyable time where we all worked hard then relaxed together in the bath afterwards, putting the world to rights and taking the piss out of each other. The big communal bath would be the social point of the dressing room with 17 blokes in it without a stitch on, reading the paper or smoking with bubbles popping up everywhere in the murky brown water and at the end of the bath. There was more water in it than when it was run, if you know what I mean. I am not sure that it's something many players today would take part in but those times were brilliant.

Another great help to me was physio Les Bardsley. Les and I had a great relationship. Being a physio is not only down to your medical expertise but you are spending time with players who are usually at their lowest ebb when injured, so you also have to be a bit of an agony uncle to them, encouraging them in their bid to get fit and instilling confidence in them. Les certainly did that for me as he saw me through some tough times when I was injured. He was a funny guy who could also be really stern, and heaven help you if you were late for one of his treatments as he would certainly give you a mouthful. He could also be extremely blunt; for instance if you came in to see him regarding what you thought was an injury he would just say, 'That's bollocks, get back out training.' But my lasting memory will always be of him usually in a white coat sat on the bench puffing away at his pipe, and if you were injured during a game and he had to come on to treat you he would get up slowly and carefully put his pipe out before running on to the field. He really was a one-off.

Another great memory is of kit man Bill Tovey. Again Bill was a funny guy who would occasionally help Les out with things like massages. Bill was not the greatest of masseurs as he would cover you with carbolic soap and proceed to grapple you to remove all the aches and pains in your legs. Most of the time he put the pain there as he would bend you up into all shapes. Bill was also our cook on away games. To save money, the club started to put a stop to overnight stays so we got a coach that had a kitchen in the back and it was nothing for Bill to cook 25 steaks along with a salad or potatoes while hurtling down the motorway at about 60 miles an hour.

I also want to mention the driver of that coach, whose name was Ray Charles. I kid you not. Ray drove us all over the country for around ten years and was a lovely man who put up with quite a lot on the coach. I remember when our keeper Ray Cashley needed to have a piss and as there was no toilet on the coach and we were running late we couldn't stop, but Cash got Ray to open the doors as we sped down the motorway and with two other lads holding Cash back he proceeded to piss out of the open door, much to our amusement and other drivers' astonishment.

But anyway, back to Bill. It was also Bill you went to to try and get any new kit or boots, which in itself was a difficult task for anyone. When I was breaking into the first team I used to love Adidas boots – they have always been my regular choice – but at the time the club gave you boots from the Co-op store. If you wanted any others you would have to pay the difference, which I did. I always got the boots from Loxtons Sports Shop on North Street in Bedminster. My boots would last and last as I would end up taking them to a repairer in Nailsea who would always put a patch across the hole where my big toe would be sticking through. Many a time the patch came off in a game and I would be playing top-flight football with my toe sticking out. In the end I would take them to Bill and he would study them intently before agreeing that I could get some new boots. I think players today change their boots every couple of games!

Thinking about the City family, there was also Beryl Fudge who was involved in the supporters' club and sold tickets and anything else she could do to help the club. Jim Evans was another great servant to Bristol City with the supporters' club and the promotions side of things. I also want to mention a real dear friend of mine, the local singer and comedian Fred Wedlock. Fred and his wife Sue were really good friends to me and Wendy. Fred was a massive Bristol City fan who had a huge hit in 1981 with 'The Oldest Swinger In Town'. He was City through and through as his relation Billy Wedlock had played over 400 games for City as well as 26 times for England during the early 1900s. As couples, we would go to parties or have dinner together and it was extremely sad when in 2010 Fred passed away with cancer. Sue rang me out of the blue and told me she was getting some stuff together for a local cancer charity and she found one of my City shirts in the pile and asked if she could let the charity have it. I said yes and if I'm honest I never thought much about it. But then she phoned a few days later and said, 'I can't let them have it, Geoff, it wouldn't be right, so you can have it back.' When it arrived it was my shirt from the promotion game against Portsmouth back in 1976. In the melee of euphoria I had apparently given it to Fred after the game and he had kept it for all those years.

Back then we never thought about memorabilia or anything like that but I'm really glad I have it now. Since getting the shirt back I have cherished it and got the rest of the team to sign it. It sits at home along with my England cap and shirt and just looking at it brings back some great memories.

All these people I now think of, including the club's secretaries over the years, helped to make this such a great family club that has had an impact on every player who has pulled on that red shirt. When I see the club today they are somewhat unrecognisable. In the years after 1982 it was very difficult for me to go to Ashton Gate again as I felt so upset by the things that had happened. There was a period where I felt completely disregarded by them; there was never an invitation to come to a game or a call to see how me and my family were. If I did take my boys to a game I would just queue up and buy my ticket to the Dolman Stand.

City have always let themselves down in that department. I recall how when Jack Connor left after 11 great years of service he used to ask me to get him a ticket as he couldn't get one through the club. But over the years I have mellowed and the club seems to have changed tack regarding ex-players and I have gone to various functions and always been treated extremely warmly by the fans and those who work at Ashton Gate. I know it's now a different club and many of the people who instigated the Ashton Gate Eight period have gone. I have been incredibly touched by the acknowledgement of our sacrifice by the new board and the Lansdown family as a whole. I believe their sentiments regarding all eight of us are genuine and I have always been very touched by the supporters' love for me. I always look for City's results and I'm always interested in what's going on down there, but I do struggle to follow today's football.

I feel I must also mention two dear friends: Dave Fear, who is sadly no longer with us, and Richard Scudamore, who until recently was chairman of the Premier League. Dave was a massive City fan and he ran an electrical business in Bristol, often doing work with the club. Richard has been a supporter all his life and on many occasions he told me about how I was his favourite player, which is very touching. A few years ago, when things were not going particularly well for me in terms of the recession in the building trade, I received a call from Dave who said he and Richard were trying to organise a celebration dinner for me at the club, which was really flattering. I thought nobody would come but I said it was a fantastic idea. Everything went quiet for a while as it turned out that the club said they couldn't have the dinner at Ashton Gate as it would set a precedent for former players in the future. It was really disappointing but Dave and Richard never gave up and in the end we had the most wonderful evening at a hotel on the outskirts of the city.

It was a lovely warm evening and there were so many people from my past such as Joe Royle, Chris Garland and the wonderful Marina Dolman. In fact I think I knew everybody who attended, many even from my younger days kicking a ball around the Marsh in Bedminster. Former City owner Scott Davidson gave a lovely speech about me and it was a really emotional evening with all my friends. It was, looking back, just what I needed at that particular time in my life and I will be forever thankful to Dave and Richard for all their hard work in making it happen.

The game today is a fast and ever-changing one and it really doesn't appeal to me, although I do enjoy watching the Leicester City and England centre-forward Jamie Vardy, who is exciting and plays with a smile on his face. I wonder if that's due to coming into professional football late and therefore seeming to appreciate it more than the normal Premier League player who has been through the academy system since the age of 12. The players today just seem to be posers, more concerned with executing the correct goal celebration than anything else. There doesn't seem to be any excitement in the modern game, and tackling is a dying art. I am also astounded by how players can cheat each other and run after the referee to get a fellow player sent off, then look the opposing player in the eye after the game.

There were more characters in football when I played and nearly every club had a couple of real stars who would produce some wonderful football on some terrible pitches, with heavy balls and heavy boots. It's also very funny that nobody appears to get muddy any more. I find it strange in today's game when I see a team is say going in at half-time 2-0 down and they are all chatting and laughing as they leave the field. They plainly don't have a John Sillett waiting for them in the dressing room. If it happened to us we would be heads down with solemn faces as we knew what was coming. But today, if players are bollocked hard by the manager or coach they will be on the phone to their agent asking for a move as they have been disrespected. I know I'm an old bloke but it's just my opinion. I just think the time I played in was a golden era in the game.

This book has also given me the opportunity to look back on players I played against and a few I played with. In terms of ability

I will never forget how good Jantzen Derrick was for City. He was so skilful that I don't think money could buy him today. Jantzen and the likes of Jack Connor helped me and guided me in my early career at City. Players like that had an aura about them; they gave me their time and showed me what was needed to become not only a player but a decent man. They had a massive influence on me. When it comes to my prime at City, I don't want to pick anybody out of the 1976 promotion side as for me there was no better group of players to be around and no better team to play in. The players who came into that team during our top-flight years, such as Royle, Hunter, Cormack and Mabbutt, were all great too and on top of their game at that time. When it comes to opponents, I would have to say that every one of those big old bruising centre-forwards I met when I first broke into the City team taught me something, but over the course of my career I have shared a pitch with many of Britain's greatest footballers. George Best, even in the testimonials we played in together, was still such a gifted player even though he was not technically in football any more. Bobby Moore will always stand out for me as a gentleman on and off the pitch, but players like Dalglish, Hoddle, Regis, Bremner, Souness and Ball were just exceptional footballers.

If I had to look back at specific players I came up against then I would have to say Derek Possee and Barry Bridges of Millwall both really gave me a hard time. They were brave and very skilful. I suppose you remember the players that gave you a challenge more. Steve Heighway of Liverpool was a top player. I remember going to slide tackle him in a game at Ashton Gate just in front of the East End, and as I slid in he did a complete u-turn and passed the ball across the box for a goal while I carried on straight into the advertising hoardings.

I recall playing against Mike Summerbee who was also very skilful and he had an aura around him because he was so cool. You have to be cool to have had George Best as your best man when you got married, as Mike did. Mike would chat with you during the game and you would think 'he's a good bloke' then he would get the ball, push it through your legs and off he would go. If Mike's skill ended in a goal or they would lose possession he would run back and give you a wink. Mike was top-drawer.

I always felt quite confident if an opponent was very vocal as this usually meant that I had the better of them. This was very much the case with Liverpool and England star Kevin Keegan. Kevin suited me no end and I don't think I had a bad game against him. As the match went on he would complain to the ref about his decisions and complain about me non-stop. I really frustrated him but afterwards he would shake my hand and say 'well done'.

I think the master of the wind-up on the field was Peter Osgood, who I knew vaguely through Chris Garland. Peter would try and wind you up all game saying you were terrible, or saying things about your wife or other players' girlfriends, although sometimes he would say something about how terrible you had been the week before and you would think, 'How the bloody hell did he know that?' Things like that never bothered me as they were all part of the game.

Trevor Francis was also a difficult player to play against. He was so quick it was untrue, and with the ball at his feet he was a remarkable player who would send you one way then go another. I also struggled with John O'Hare, who was at Derby County and Nottingham Forest. John was tough and like a barrel; he was so difficult to get near it was untrue. He had unbelievable power both in his running and his shooting. I remember being at a Bristol City dinner once where the guest speaker was the legendary manager Brian Clough. He took great delight in telling the audience that City's best player (apparently me) could not get near John O'Hare. The game in question was around 1979, a 1-1 draw at Ashton Gate. In my defence I was suffering terribly with the flu and wasn't even going to play, but yes O'Hare was great that day, although I am extremely flattered that Clough thought I was the best player at Ashton Gate.

Talking of Clough, I have played against many great sides such as the Leeds United side of the 1970s and Liverpool's European conquerors, but the best team was Clough's Nottingham Forest of the late 1970s. Although they never battered us in any game they were the quickest in terms of passing and speed through the pitch that I had ever seen. With players like Robertson, McGovern, O'Neill, and Woodcock, their passing and movement was better than anyone, from Shilton in goal through to Birtles up front.

Football has given me some tough times and some wonderful times over the years. On reflection I would rather concentrate on the wonderful times I had. I was captain of my country as a schoolboy, I joined my boyhood club, I captained them all the way to the top flight and led them out into the First Division. I have travelled all over the world and played the game I love in many different countries from the USA to the townships of South Africa. Football has enabled me to meet so many people from all walks of life, whether I have played at Anfield or Old Trafford, or turned out with my two sons at Nailsea Town with a pint after the match. I have loved football all my life and I have given everything to it. My story is one of ups and downs in football and also in life.

This has been my life with the Robins and beyond and I have loved sharing it with you.

17

Geoff

I NEVER really knew Geoff socially but on the field he was a tough, honest pro. I use the term honest as he would tackle you and give you some stick and if you gave it back there was no problem. I always associate him with that great Bristol City team of the 1970s. Geoff was in that classic partnership at the back of one big one and one smaller one. He would be partnered by Dave Rodgers or Gary Collier, and Geoff being the smaller one would be like lightning over the pitch, clearing up any problem. He was a top player.

Phil Bater

Bristol Rovers, Wrexham, Brentford, Cardiff City 1974–1989

Geoff Merrick was one of the greatest defenders I ever played against and I certainly played against a few. He was a class act who was quick and had incredible timing in the air. He had an ability to guide you where he wanted you to go and wouldn't dive into the tackle. He would get you when he knew he could. He always played well against us at Wolves and I remember our manager Bill

McGarry at the time asking me what I thought of Geoff. I told him I thought he was class and we should push the boat out and sign him. Bill rated him so highly that he wanted to bring him to Molineux as captain. I think we made offers but nothing came of it. He would have been brilliant for us.

John Richards

Wolverhampton Wanderers, Derby County 1969–1983

I remember Geoff; he was a real gentleman. I played against him many times and if my memory serves me right I always did well against him. That does not take away the fact that I always had to be on top of my game when facing him. He was quick and read the game expertly. I always thought he would go on and play for one of the big clubs at some point in his career.

Derek Possee

Millwall, Crystal Palace, Leyton Orient 1967–1977

Geoff Merrick, well he was a top defender. I played against him many times with various clubs and I don't think I had so much as a kick. He was not the sort of defender who tried to intimidate you; if anything he was quiet but he read the game so well and was so composured on the ball it was unreal. He reminded me of Bobby Moore and that's the best compliment I can pay him.

Ted MacDougall

York City, Bournemouth, Manchester United, West Ham United, Norwich City, Southampton, Blackpool 1967–1980

I came up through the ranks with Geoff at Bristol City. I always respected him as a player and a man. He was our captain and he led by example. He would be vocal in the dressing room, especially if things were not going well.

We shared some great times and unfortunately some awful ones, in particular the Ashton Gate Eight episode. All the way through that time he was still our captain, taking a lot of the pressure off us and putting it on to his own shoulders. He became our spokesman and I'm honoured to still call him a friend to this day.

Trevor Tainton

Bristol City, Torquay United 1965–1982

I remember coming to Bristol City and meeting Geoff for the first time. He was quiet but what he did say you took notice of. He was only young when he got the captaincy and he blossomed in the role. He was a tremendous player and he led by example. He is a gentleman off the pitch also. I'm honoured to have played with him.

John Galley

Wolverhampton Wanderers, Rotherham United, Bristol City, Nottingham Forest, Peterborough United, Hereford United 1961–1977

I had the honour of playing for Bristol Boys with Geoff. You could see he was going to make a great player at the age of 11. Such a stylish left-sided player. I really enjoyed playing behind him in goal. You could not wish to meet a nicer sportsman.

Steve Sutor

Friend

Geoff was always a gentleman both on and off the field. I remember he came into the first team at a young age, and nothing fazed him. He was a great captain for the club and a player you could depend on. I have the utmost respect for him.

Mike Gibson

Bristol City 1963–1972

My initial experience with Geoff was from a competitive point of view as he was Bristol City and I was Rovers. And I have to say he was a very well-respected opponent. He was a defender of pure class. Every time I played against him he delivered a high level of performance and for the Rovers strikers at the time he gave nothing away, and you would come away from the game thinking he really is top-drawer.

He was a great reader of the game who not only did his own work but looked after other players around him, which can be a rare commodity in the game. You would always have to be at your best to get anything over on Geoff. When I played with him, although he suffered with injuries he was a big influence on everybody around him due to his stature at the club. He gave his heart and soul to the club and was Bristol City through and through and the thought that he would leave for another club was unthinkable. Unfortunately the way it finished for him was terrible. If you had to say somebody did not deserve that it would have to be Geoff. It wasn't the case for me as I had not been at the club long and I had been at Rovers but Geoff certainly did not deserve the way it ended for him. He will always be a Bristol City legend and a gentleman.

Peter Aitken

Bristol Rovers, Bristol City, York City 1972–1982

Geoff was a great leader for Bristol City. He was calm and would give encouragement while also having that ability to get at you when it was needed. The best captain I ever played with and certainly one of the best defenders. Throughout the whole Ashton Gate Eight period he would also be there for us with advice and encouragement. A top man.

Jimmy Mann

Leeds United, Bristol City, Barnsley, Scunthorpe United, Doncaster Rovers 1969–1983

Geoff was a Bedminster boy like myself. I remember Geoff making his debut in the 1968/69 season and I knew he was going to be a City legend. Quick, tenacious, good in the air and he possessed a clever footballing brain.

Jantzen Derrick

Bristol City, Paris Saint-Germain 1959–1972

Geoff Merrick is one of football's good guys. I first played against him at youth team level when I was at Swindon Town. He has always been a top defender who played the game the right way. We had battles but he always offered a handshake at the end. I recall helping him with a hip injury during his career. I don't think anyone at Bristol City had a clue as to the cause but I had the same injury months earlier and I remember contacting him about it and giving him the name of the surgeon who worked on me. I think it was a weight off his mind at the time. I have always thought that it was a loss that he never played for England as in my opinion he was definitely international class.

Mike Summerbee

Swindon Town, Manchester City, Burnley, Blackpool, Stockport County 1959–1979

I have great affection for Geoff. I liked him from the moment I first met him when we were in the England Schoolboys side together. In all the games he was Mr Consistency and as our captain he was the one to look up to. They were great days. We were all working-class kids and we stayed in some fantastic hotels during our England time. Geoff was a great player who you knew would go on to play at the top flight even though that rarely happens with the England Schoolboys. He was brave and he could read a game even at that young age, and when he spoke we listened. I played against him many times with all my different clubs and it's been fantastic through Neil and this book to be reunited with him after all these years. Looking back, I'm sure he would have fitted in with any of the big clubs during the 1970s and even would have gone on to play for England. He really is a gentleman.

Dave Thomas

Burnley, QPR, Everton, Wolverhampton Wanderers, Middlesbrough, Portsmouth 1966–1984

I remember Geoff when I arrived at Bristol City as a youngster. He was the rising star, and he was somebody we looked up to and followed. He led by example and when he became captain of the side, he just had an aura about him. I eventually played with him and I'm proud to have shared a pitch with him and to call him a friend.

Tom Ritchie

Bristol City, Sunderland, Carlisle United 1969–1984

I remember my debut for Bristol City in the 1973/74 season. It was against Leyton Orient. We lost 2-0. The game was on the Saturday and we had training on the Monday, then after it we all went to one of the club's lounges to watch a recording of the game and dissect it with Alan Dicks. Geoff scored an own goal for the first goal, which he could do nothing about. For the second goal full-back Brian Drysdale told Geoff he was going forward to attack the man with the ball. What he should have done was fill Brian's space but he didn't and as a result Leyton Orient scored the second. Anyway I said in the meeting that Geoff was at fault, which he didn't like. He actually said, 'You can't speak to me like that, I'm the captain,' to which I replied, 'I couldn't care less who you are, it's your fault so admit it.' I had been at Norwich City under manager Ron Saunders who believed in saying things as they were and it rubbed off on me. Some players sided with Geoff and some with me and it got quite heated. In the end Alan Dicks told us all to go home.

After that, every time I did something wrong in training Geoff would tell me, which in hindsight made me a better player. That first meeting meant we had a real respect for each other which stayed with us. He was a great captain who always looked after the lads, and he would also challenge Alan Dicks if he thought something was wrong, which earned the respect of all the players. Geoff Merrick is an honest, tough player who really could play. He was also a real club man who gave everything for his team-mates.

Paul Cheesley

Norwich City, Bristol City 1971–1976

Geoff always had a presence about him and I think he could have managed in any sort of industry as he would command respect from people. When I joined City in 1972 he was a very young captain, he never shouted or called out people but he was not frightened of giving you some stick if he thought it would make you a better player. He had a great left foot and his heading was tremendous considering he wasn't that big. He was Bristol City through and through and everybody at the club from top to bottom respected him.

Clive Whitehead

Bristol City, West Bromwich Albion, Wolverhampton Wanderers, Portsmouth, Exeter City 1972–1990

I never saw Geoff play but my dad always talked about what a great player he was. When I became captain of the club it was Geoff Merrick who set the standard of how a Bristol City captain should behave, on the pitch and off it. The role off the pitch was being the face of Bristol City and going out and meeting the fans at various events. I know this was something that Geoff did and I made sure I carried on that tradition. I always thought of him as Mr Bristol City and a great asset to the club. It was always my dream to do what he did and that was to be a local lad, which I was, and lead my home town club out in the top flight of football. I came close in 2008 with our play-off final defeat against Hull City but that's why Geoff is so special to us all as he did it. I have met him on numerous occasions and he really is a great bloke who was a massive part of this club.

Louis Carey

Bristol City, Coventry City, Bristol City 1995-2014

If it wasn't for the likes of Geoff Merrick and seven other players I certainly would not have had the career in football that I had. I owe them everything. When I was an apprentice at Bristol City I looked up to Geoff and he always acknowledged us youngsters and asked us how we were getting on. It would make us feel ten feet tall. He would also give advice and we all listened. He tore up his contract through no fault of his own, losing his career and money to save the club. That then allowed people like me to get my start in the game. When I became captain at the club I would always think, 'What would Geoff do in this situation?' He was a massive influence on me and his sacrifice for the club should never be forgotten.

The game is vastly different now and I see that every day in my job as head of Manchester City's recruitment of players. The game is awash with money and the values and decency that somebody like Geoff Merrick had are a fading memory in the modern game. He will always be somebody I look up to with the utmost respect.

Rob Newman
Bristol City, Norwich City, Motherwell, Wigan Athletic, Southend United 1981–2002

I remember when I came to City, there were lots of older pros and I wanted to move the club on and that meant playing the likes of Geoff Merrick. I liked him as a player and a youngster. When I gave him his debut at Aston Villa in the 1968 season, he was 17 but I had no worries that he would grow as a player. I later made him captain as a 20-year-old and he never let me down.

Geoff could read the game brilliantly and his jump was second to none. He also possessed one of the best left feet I had seen. He was a great captain; quiet and thoughtful, never just shouting the odds in the dressing room for no reason. When he spoke, the lads all listened. Don't get me wrong, he would challenge me at times and I respected him for it as his point of view was always well thought out. He took the role of captain seriously and with pride, travelling to many different functions and events across Bristol as the club's representative at times and that was great to see.

When I moved Geoff to left-back due to the arrival of Norman Hunter he wasn't pleased but to his credit he got on with things and he did exceptionally well in that role. Geoff is a fighter who never gave me too many problems when I was manager, apart from the time he came to see me and asked if it was okay for him to take his heavy goods licence test as he might need a licence to drive vehicles on the farm. I was taken aback and said, 'I'm not really happy with you doing that, Geoff, as I want you to concentrate on football and I don't want you having an accident.' I thought he should do it when he retired.

I must also add that I firmly believe that Geoff kept me in a job during the 1973/74 season. We were struggling in the league and I found out, some years later, that chairman Harry Dolman had said to the board that he was going to the West Indies on holiday and when he got back he did not expect Alan Dicks to be at Ashton Gate. While Harry was away we went to

Hereford in the FA Cup fourth round and won 1-0 with Geoff getting the vital goal. A few days later we drew First Division Leeds United and beat them at Elland Road in a replay. After that cup run, which ended with defeat against Liverpool in the next round, my job was safe. We both shared some great times at Bristol City and some low times, but I want to say thank you Geoff for everything.

Alan Dicks

Bristol City manager 1967–1980

I have known Geoff for many years and although we played for the different Bristol clubs I always thought he had an aura about him, much like Bobby Moore did. I played against him many times and he was always a fair but tough opponent, but I really got to know him when Geoff came to Bristol Rovers for a season in the reserves when I was the youth team coach. He was magnificent with the young lads. He gave them advice and his play on the pitch was second to none. I would always say to the lads, 'Just watch Geoff and you won't go wrong.' He was brilliant for us that year and his influence on all the young players was much appreciated by all the coaching staff. He finished his career early and it was a sad loss to the game as I'm sure he would have made a great coach, but I think the experience he went through at City scarred him from the game. He will always be a City legend.

Harold Jarman

Bristol Rovers, Newport County 1959–1974

I played with Geoff from youth team to first team. He was a natural leader who always led by example. He was confident and calm on the ball and as a keeper that is just what you need in front of you. All the way through his career he never changed despite the limelight of being the club's captain in the top division. He really is a great bloke, and we shared some great times together.

Ray Cashley

Bristol City, Hereford United, Bristol Rovers, 1969–1981

I remember playing against Geoff many times during my career. I seem to recall I did okay against Bristol City while I was at Birmingham City, Nottingham Forest and Manchester City. I'm not sure that was due to Geoff or not but I do remember that he was a top professional who was honest, quick and was surprisingly good in the air for somebody who was not that tall. He always gave me a good game all the way through my career. But it was at the start of my career that I first met Geoff; he probably won't remember it but I do. I was from Plymouth and I got invited to Bristol City along with my mate Kevin Griffin. We both came up to Ashton Gate for a week's trial. It would have been about 1968 as I was 15 years old. I recall the first team had the likes of John Galley and Chris Garland in the side. I was mainly playing with the reserves and I recall being thrilled when I was asked to travel with the reserves by coach to Stamford Bridge for a game against Chelsea. Geoff was on that coach and he was very much the rising star at the club. City were keen on both me and Kevin but I had already promised Birmingham that I was going to go up and see them. In the end Kevin signed for Bristol City as an apprentice and made a few appearances for them before moving on to Bath City. I signed for Birmingham and the rest as they say is history. It's strange to think that me and Geoff could have been team-mates if things had been different, but that's football. I wish Geoff every success with the book.

Trevor Francis

Birmingham City, Nottingham Forest, Manchester City, Sampdoria, Atalanta, Glasgow Rangers, Queens Park Rangers, Sheffield Wednesday, England 1969–1994

I first met Geoff when I arrived at Ashton Gate in 1969 from Hartlepool United. We hit it off straight away as we both had the same sense of humour and although I was on my own at the time he welcomed me into his extended family, meeting his mum and dad who were wonderful people. Geoff used to room with Chris Garland and I roomed with Dickie Rooks but when Chris left for Chelsea and Dickie went to Willington FC in the north-east the natural thing was for me and Geoff to room together, which we did. He was a great player and it was a privilege playing with him. We used to laugh through games at times, particularly if we were under pressure. I'm sure the opposing forwards thought we were mad. It was the same at training; although we took it seriously we would always get a telling off from John Sillett for mucking about on cross-country runs. Over the years Geoff and his lovely family have been wonderful friends to myself and my family and it's an honour to call him a friend. He is a real Bristol City legend.

Brian Drysdale

Lincoln City, Hartlepool United, Bristol City, Reading, Oxford United 1960–1978

When I arrived at Ashton Gate, Ken Wimshurst was captain and as Ken was moving into coaching there was a space for somebody to take up the mantle. There was a lot of people saying that Geoff was too young at 20 but Alan Dicks decided Geoff was the man and it was a great appointment for us. He took the role seriously both on and off the field; you could tell it meant so much to him. He was more refined than the rest of us. We would have a laugh, as would Geoff, but we would take it too far and invariably Geoff would watch and have a word with us to calm things down.

Geoff was a great player who handled things well both on the pitch and off the pitch with the media. He proved his worth in games; he was a great winner of the ball and a great user of it, he leapt in the air as though he had springs in his ankles and he never lost many battles in the air, that's for sure. Geoff was a natural leader and that was never more evident than when we went through the Ashton Gate Eight saga together. We were all dumbfounded by the request to rip up our contracts and we had nobody to guide us, but even though Geoff was under great pressure like the rest of us he took things on to his shoulders and contacted the PFA and started to mobilise things for us. He is a wonderful bloke who could have played higher but he stayed loyal to Bristol City as they were his club.

Gerry Sweeney

Bristol City, York City 1971–1982

It's a delight to say a few words about Geoff Merrick. I only played against him a few times but he was certainly one of the best defenders I have ever faced in my career and there have been many from all over the world. I don't say that lightly but I never got much from him when we faced each other. He wasn't that big but he had a great leap; he was also brilliant at reading the game and would anticipate what I was going to do before I did it. My game was to stay on the defender's shoulder and use my pace to out-sprint him but with Geoff he stayed off me and matched me for pace every time.

It's no disrespect to Bristol City as at the time they were in the top flight but I could never understand why he never moved to a bigger club as I'm sure he would have gone from strength to strength. I understand at the start of his career Liverpool were trying to buy him and I know that they would have loved him up there as he gave everything. I wish Geoff all the best for the future and especially with this book.

Kevin Keegan

Scunthorpe United, Liverpool, Hamburg, Southampton, Newcastle United, England 1968–1984

I first met Geoff Merrick when I was an apprentice at Bristol City round about 1973. Me and the rest of the apprentices were in awe of him as he was very much the main man at Ashton Gate. The thing was though he was great with all the young lads, always giving us advice and making himself available to us if we wanted a chat. He never left anybody out, which was a mark of a great captain. I really got to know him both on the field and sociably when I broke into the first team aged 18. Geoff was a great player with a fantastic left foot, and he had a great leap which deceived many forwards as he wasn't that big. I roomed with him for a few years and he helped me enormously as I strived to become a player with advice, etc.

I remember some great times with Geoff, especially when on a tour of America with the club. He and Chris Garland drove me and another youngster, Shaun Penny, down to the beach at Palm Springs for the day. They were both established players and here they were taking two youngsters out for the day. They looked upon us as part of the team irrespective of the fact that we had not made many appearances.

I also recall when Alan Dicks moved him from his better position of alongside a big centre-half in the back four to full-back due to the arrival of Norman Hunter. Geoff never wanted to play at full-back but he just got on with things for the benefit of the club and he sent a message out that the club was everything to him. After he was sacked at City we met up again in later life when we were both playing for Nailsea Town. We had some great times and although me and Geoff never saw eye to eye sometimes as we both wanted to win so badly, after the games we would have a pint in the pub with his two boys, who also played for Nailsea, and have the time of our lives. You could see how much he enjoyed the camaraderie of Nailsea. Overall he's a lovely man off the field and one of Bristol City's greatest players on it.

Howard Pritchard

Bristol City, Swindon Town, Gillingham, Walsall, Maidstone United 1976–1990

It's an honour and privilege to pay tribute to Geoff. A captain and leader of men and a top-quality defender and Bristol City icon. I was most impressed with his leadership in my first big challenge as the new CEO of the PFA and tasked with the survival of the club and the sacrifice of the Ashton Gate Eight. Following this sacrifice we introduced the football creditor rule which has stood the test of time and ensured the protection of the players whenever clubs have had to go into administration and look for new owners. As a Bristol boy, the city is in debt to him for his contribution as a player and the survival as well as triumphs of Bristol City Football Club.

Gordon Taylor OBE

Professional Footballers' Association

I remember Geoff when he was captain of Bristol Boys and of course England Schoolboys. Throughout his career he has always been a great captain, in particular at Bristol City. You could tell that he loved the football club and he was a fantastic ambassador on and off the field. Although he was cheeky at times he carried himself like a captain and I remember when Harry and I would have the players up to our house pre-season to play bowls or tennis then give them afternoon tea, Geoff was always so polite and respectful. Harry thought an awful lot of him and I will certainly never forget what he, along with the seven other players, did for this club by cancelling their contracts. I love both him and Wendy. They are a wonderful couple and I know what this football club means to Geoff. He is a very special man and a dear friend and I wish him well with this book.

Marina Dolman MBE

President of Bristol City FC

I first met Geoff when we were schoolboys in the Bristol Boys under-15 team. Geoff was 15 but I was 14 and we have remained friends ever since. He is without doubt the best footballer I have ever played with. Sometimes he never had to tackle an opponent, he would guide them into an area he wanted them to go and before they realised it they were in a dead end. He would also run into the space that a forward wanted to get into. It was called reading the game and he was a master at it.

I always felt he could have played at a higher level but Geoff was really loyal to the club. As a captain he was magnificent and you could see what it meant to him and that rubbed off on all the lads in the team. He wasn't vociferous, he just led by example, which was always with a clear head. Although we don't see each other enough, when we do get together it's just like those City days gone by. He and Wendy are a lovely couple and I'm proud to call them my friends.

Keith Fear

Bristol City, Hereford United, Blackburn Rovers, Plymouth Argyle, Brentford, Chester, Wimbledon 1969–1981

Over the years I have been privileged to have known both Geoff the footballer and Geoff the man. Geoff the footballer is the number one reason that I became hooked on football and in particular Bristol City. My father took me to games at Ashton Gate in the late 1960s. Geoff was a youngster and in and out of the team at the time but there was something about him that I liked. Then all of a sudden he became an ever-present in the side. I was about 12 years of age and my dad, who was disabled, had one of those disability vehicles so it meant we could come to the games and park right on the side of the pitch. I remember I would keep on at Dad that we had to get to the game early so we could see Geoff's warm-up, which was almost pre-match entertainment for me. He would leap constantly into the air like a salmon over and over again. I was mesmerised by him. He was always the number one player for me.

Then I got to know him as a man through our mutual friend, the now sadly departed Dave Fear. Geoff is everything you expect him to be; he was immaculate on the field, always in control and a very solid, talented player. Off the pitch he had all those qualities while also being modest, strong and unassuming. He has a professionalism about him and he's just a super guy. A few years ago Dave Fear and myself organised a dinner in honour of him, which was well received by supporters. It raised a few quid for Geoff, which was great, but it was nothing compared to the pleasure he gave us all over the years in that red shirt.

Richard Scudamore

Chairman of the Premier League 2014–2018

Bristol City fan for life

About the Author

GEOFF MERRICK has collaborated with friend and writer Neil Palmer to tell his story. Neil has written for various sports publications and websites over the years. Based in Bristol, Neil has written 11 books to date, including the popular *Derby Days* series which looked at the Bristol derby and the Welsh derby, along with *The Trevor Ford Story*, the biography of the Welsh football maverick of the 1950s. Neil has also written *He's Here, He's There*, the critically acclaimed biography of Bristol City legend Gerry Gow, which was released in 2021.